John Dankworth

Sax from the Start

Kevin
Mayhew

First published in 1996 by
KEVIN MAYHEW LTD
Rattlesden
Bury St Edmunds
Suffolk IP30 0SZ

0 1 2 3 4 5 6 7 8 9

ISBN 0 86209 901 3
Catalogue No 3611214

Front cover photograph courtesy of Pictor International Ltd, London.

Photography by Bruce Head
Typesetting by Louise Hill
Music setting by Donald Thomson
Printed and bound in Great Britain by
Caligraving Limited Thetford Norfolk

CONTENTS

INTRODUCTION

If you're able to read this sentence you're a potential saxophone player. And any potential saxophone player is a potential virtuoso, even a potential star.

Not that playing the saxophone is any easier than any other musical instrument. (Well – it may be easier than some, but there again it's harder than others.) Nevertheless I've always maintained that anybody with minimal skills and even with only a small amount of natural musical ability can, with enough effort, be a good saxophone player. And that includes you.

So take each step slowly and thoroughly. Don't be tempted to race ahead faster than you can take it all in. I can't predict the speed with which you'll achieve any one step. Some things will come more easily than others but rest assured that if you feel stuck on something you find difficult, there'll be someone somewhere in the world having a difficult time with something you found easy. So don't get despondent. Or, if you do, rest assured that I who have been playing the darned thing for countless years, still occasionally get depressed when my saxophone won't do what I want it to!

Still, the pleasure you'll get when the instrument does obey your orders, and eventually begins to make some beautiful sounds at your command, will far outweigh the problems you faced in the earlier days. So don't stop trying, and sooner or later you'll reach the point when you pat yourself on the back and say to yourself, 'Well – I never thought I'd get this far'.

So enjoy your journey into the new world of saxophone playing. You've joined a legion of people millions strong all over the world who share the joys, the frustrations, the problems and the rewards of playing this exhilarating instrument.

Welcome to the club!

JOHN DANKWORTH

SELECTING AN INSTRUMENT

1 Soprano saxophone

3 Tenor saxophone

2 Alto saxophone

4 Baritone saxophone

Choosing a saxophone for the first time can be a problem, but not an insurmountable one. There are plenty of ways of finding someone to help you.

Some music stores who stock saxophones may not have sales staff who know a great deal about the instrument. Find a store with someone there who does – that's the first step. Ask them for advice on the type of saxophone. There are several choices – soprano, alto, tenor or baritone being the most likely *(see Figures 1 - 4)*. The baritone is a much used instrument in the saxophone world, but its size makes it perhaps not the most suitable to learn on. But all saxophones have more or less identical fingering, so whatever type you start on needn't be the one you commit yourself to for life! You can quite well learn on a soprano or alto, and later decide you'd like to switch to the tenor. That's no problem at all – in fact many professionals play several types, although some of the most famous players in the history of the instrument have tended to specialise in, and stick with, just one of the types.

If the assistants in the store can play, let them demonstrate the instruments for you. Don't be rushed into making your mind up – in fact any reputable music sales assistant will not want to hurry you into a wrong decision anyway.

If you have difficulty in finding a place where someone has an intimate knowledge of saxophones, try to get someone to go with you on your shopping expedition who knows a bit about it. But if all these attempts to involve someone knowledgeable fail, don't despair; you should still be able to go ahead by yourself if you buy at a reputable store.

First Preparations

We'll presume that at last you've got your instrument home. Well, now's the magic moment when you put it together.

Some musical instruments come in a

5

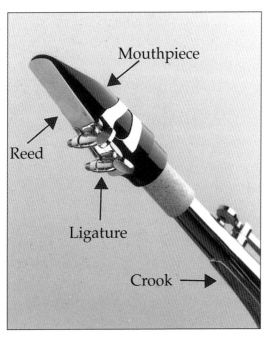

6

number of pieces and are a bit of a jigsaw puzzle to assemble. But the saxophone comes in, at the most, two pieces – the *crook* and the *body (see Figure 5)*, so it doesn't take a genius to put it all together. And sopranos are usually made in one piece, so they come ready to add the mouthpiece and play.

Once the instrument is assembled it is ready to receive . . .

The mouthpiece (see Figure 6) which is the 'nerve centre' of the saxophone as it is with every 'blowing' instrument. It is the source of all the sounds which we will shortly be getting from our sax. The mouthpiece will, however, make no musical sounds by itself. These sounds are produced in conjunction with . . .

The reed, a flat piece of very thin cane which is placed on the mouthpiece and caused to vibrate. The reed makes the sound in the same way as a piece of tissue paper folded over a haircomb makes a sound when blown and hummed into – well, nearly the same way, that is! But more of that in a moment. The reed is held on to the mouthpiece by . . .

The ligature, a device which acts as a sort of clamp to keep the reed in the right position, so that the 'business end' of the reed (the part which gets very thin indeed at the end – careful you don't stub it!) is held over the oblong-shaped hole on the bottom of the mouthpiece. It should fit perfectly, with the tip exactly matching the end of the mouthpiece. When you're absolutely sure this is so, then tighten the ligature just enough to keep the reed in place firmly, but not enough to dig into the wood. This operation can be done either before or after putting the mouthpiece where it belongs on the cork-covered end of the instrument. It's perhaps easier to put the mouthpiece on first when you're starting, because coaxing it on to the cork is sometimes hard at first (use a little joint grease or Vaseline to ease the way if it is) and the operation may disturb or damage the reed you've just taken so much trouble to get in the right position. You should anyway have a mouthpiece cover to put on the mouthpiece to avoid this.

If you find all this very daunting it may relieve you to know that when you put your saxophone back in its case (thoroughly cleaned, of course – see page 27) you can take off the crook, leaving the mouthpiece where it is (with its cover on, of course), so that setting up to play won't take so long next time. (For soprano-sax players this won't apply, however – you'll have to remove the mouthpiece every time you put the sax away, although the mouthpiece itself can still stay assembled.)

More about Reeds

I've already said that reeds are the source of the saxophone sound. The thickness of the reed dictates the way it vibrates on the mouthpiece, and different players use widely varying strengths of reeds, which are available in many varieties. Most beginners find it easier to cope with a soft reed, so it's advisable to make sure you have a supply of very soft reeds at first. You'll find out why later. Reeds are graded 1 (softest) to 5 (hardest), and I suggest two or three of each grade 1, 1$\frac{1}{2}$ and 2 to begin with.

Plastic-coated wooden reeds and indeed reeds made entirely of plastic are on the market, and some professionals use them. But as most of the better players whom I know still prefer the old-fashioned cane reeds I suggest you start following the same path, until you are knowledgeable enough about your own requirements to try the others.

Wooden (cane) reeds can also be made softer or harder (more flexible or otherwise at the tip) by hand. A reed cutter (available at many music stores) will slice a tiny curve-shaped shaving off the tip of your reed to make it, in effect, harder. The amount you cut off will determine how much harder. And a reed can be softened by gentle scraping with sandpaper or a razor-blade on the top surface near the tip to reduce the thickness of the cane. But some players go through their careers without ever trying or even approving of these 'home industry' methods of reed improvement, and leave it all to the manufacturers by only using reeds which suit them brand-new and unaltered.

Mouthpieces also come in different adjustments of 'lay' (the table on which the reed is placed). The depth of this lay governs the amount of space the reed has to vibrate in the first place and so affects the ease of blowing. The area inside the mouthpiece, or tone chamber, also affects that sound.

Some mouthpieces are made of metal and some of plastic or similar man-made materials, and while some players contend that this has an effect on the sound produced, others disagree. It's sufficient to say that at the beginner's stage it won't make much difference either way except for the feel in the mouth. If you have a metal mouthpiece and it feels uncomfortable to you, then by all means try the other type when you can – or vice versa. It's important to feel right at the early stages.

ACT ONE – Session 1
First Sounds

7

8

Now it's nearly time to blow.

But hold on just a little bit longer. Two more things have to be done.

You'll need your sax sling or strap. (If your sax is a soprano you can do without the support a strap gives you – it's up to you.) Put the strap over your head and adjust the length of it so that its hook goes through the eyehole on the back of the instrument. Then make sure that the mouthpiece will go easily up to your mouth while the weight of the sax is taken up by the strap. This will, when correct, leave your hands free to touch the keys without having to hold up the instrument. The only non-playing job is for the right-hand thumb, which holds the sax away from the body in a good playing position. Practise this position with your hands in the position shown in the picture *(see Figure 7)* but don't put the mouthpiece in your mouth. Don't even take the mouthpiece cover off yet. You may damage that precious reed.

Now unhook the instrument and put it down.

Take off the mouthpiece cover.

Now undo the ligature, take off the reed and do what every professional player does before playing a 'cold' instrument. Put the reed in your mouth and thoroughly dampen it with saliva. A dry reed is unreliable, prone to 'squeaking' and will make your task as a beginner doubly difficult. Once your reed is well 'soaked' you can carefully replace it and the mouthpiece cover. Then once again put the saxophone on the sling and get into playing position.

Important. Merely steady the instrument with your hands. Both thumbs should be in position *(see Figure 8)* at the back of the saxophone, and the fingers must not be pressing down or activating any keys. This is very important, as any keys being pressed at this stage will stop your first sounds from emerging! If you find it hard to steady the sax without pressing any keys at first, rest the bottom of the sax on a cushion or bed so that you can concentrate better on the job in

9

Please be aware that all saxophones are transposing *instruments, and the notes written for saxophone throughout this book do* not *correspond with the same notes on a keyboard.*

hand instead of trying to control a wobbly saxophone!

Once you are sure you aren't touching or pressing any keys take off the mouthpiece cover, and put the mouthpiece close to your mouth.

This is it!

Insert the mouthpiece (with the reed at the bottom) into your mouth. Make a cushion for the reed to rest on by pulling your lower lip back into your mouth over your lower teeth.

Then do the same with your upper lip and teeth, although if you wish your upper teeth to rest on top of the mouthpiece, this is quite normal and many players (perhaps most) use this method. But certainly at this stage either way will do *(see Figure 9).*

Put the mouthpiece in until about half of the beak is in your mouth.

Then blow . . .

If you make an almost unbearable sound, don't be dismayed. You've won the first battle. Many people start by not getting anything at all! But try again, and again – and again after that. Gradually, little by little, you'll learn how to refine and improve the sound.

If you can't seem to get a sound at all, you're probably trying too hard. Just imagine that you're jamming a rubber hosepipe on to the mouthpiece instead of your mouth – and blow again. We'll go into refinement later, but the important thing now is to get some sort of noise out of the thing. (It's best during this initial period not to have too many loved ones around, and to keep away from walls or windows that adjoin neighbours' property.)

But little by little you'll learn to get the note more reliably, more steadily, more in tune and, above all, for longer periods. Keep trying to lengthen the duration of the note, and to improve its sound. The note, by the way, is

C♯

When you've achieved some sort of reliability, try making a neater start and finish to the note. Put your tongue on the end of the reed (this will stop it vibrating) and imagine yourself saying 'ta' as you begin blowing. Then put your tongue back when you want to finish the note, and, of course, stop blowing.

That'll do for the moment. But you've played a note – you're already a saxophone player.

Act One – Session 2
More Notes

So far you've learned how to play one note. So if you can already read music you would have no difficulty playing the following:

but if you haven't learned the rules of musical notation, you'll have to do a bit of extra study (see Appendix on page 124).

But it's time to learn some new notes – quite a few in fact.

Firstly, just blow the note you already know. Then starting with the first finger of the left hand, slowly put the fingers down and press the keys one by one. You will get a sort of scale going lower and lower until you run out of breath or you lose the note through lack of control.

The notes look on paper much as you'd imagine from what your fingers are doing on the instrument *(see Figures 10 - 17)*.

C♯

11

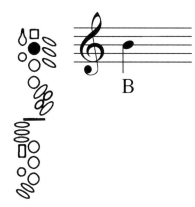

B

12

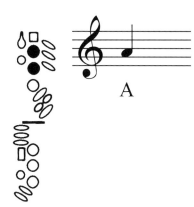

A

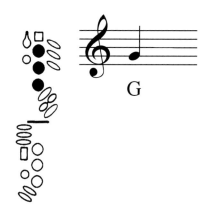

G

13

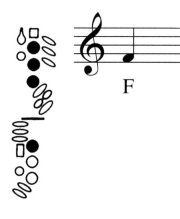

F

14

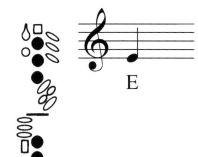

E

15

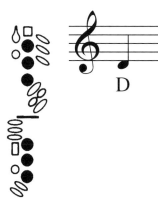

D

16

17

C

The last note is the hardest, partly because you'll be short of breath by now, and partly because of the relative weakness of the smallest finger, but if you keep at it you'll get all the notes down to the lowest in a single breath. (The right thumb merely holds the sax up, and the left is only involved in coaxing higher notes out of your instrument, which we'll come to later.)

Keep working at these notes. You'll gradually get more sure of them and improve the sound. Keep looking at yourself in a mirror as you play. The act of sax-playing should not look ugly. If you're expanding your cheeks too far you're probably doing something wrong. If your jaw is in an unnatural position you're probably straining too much.

Try playing the notes as long as possible. Time yourself on each one and try to make every one last five seconds. At this stage always start from the top notes and gradually work your way downwards.

Breathing is a study in itself and a tremendously important function of the body. If you play a wind instrument you need to know a lot about breath control. But at the moment just imagine your chest to be a toothpaste tube. The correct way to squeeze toothpaste out is to squeeze at the very end of the tube in an upwards direction.

The same applies to breathing. The air should be squeezed from the bottom by the lower muscles of the abdomen and the diaphragm. This will ensure a steady stream of air coming up to 'drive' the air column into the instrument, and help you to avoid those embarrassing 'dry-ups' which happen a great deal during the early days of learning the saxophone. More of this later.

SWAY & SWING

Interesting Note

In music, longer is lower, shorter is sharper, or higher.

'So what?' you say.

Well, it's the reason why the long strings at the bottom end of the piano (take the lid off one and look if you can) make the low notes and the short ones at the top make the high ones.

In the same way a long column of air makes a low sound. So that when you put more and more fingers down after your first note, you're making the air you're blowing go a longer and longer journey down your saxophone before it can escape through an open hole (it only comes out of the bell at the end when you play the very bottom note).

So now you're beginning to know not only how your sax works but why it works too!

ACT ONE – Session 3
Consolidation

Well, you've already reached a stage where you can actually play the saxophone. You've made some sounds which should convince you that with some really hard work you can be a good player. But before we go on to the next steps we must be sure that you really understand what's been going on so that we can make the most of the knowledge you've acquired.

So far you've learned these notes

Now our next task is to know this information thoroughly and perfectly. A computer won't work correctly unless every key you put down, every move you make, is the right one. A saxophone is the same. Test yourself all the time by playing the finger positions and visualising or writing down the note each one serves. Do them out of order and at random (don't worry if you miss some of the notes when you blow or get a bad sound – so long as you're sure the fingering is correct; your accuracy and skill will improve). But make sure you can see a 'black crow on the telephone wires' for every fingering you make, so that from now on I can refer to those notes in the sign language known as musical notation.

TEST – complete the following

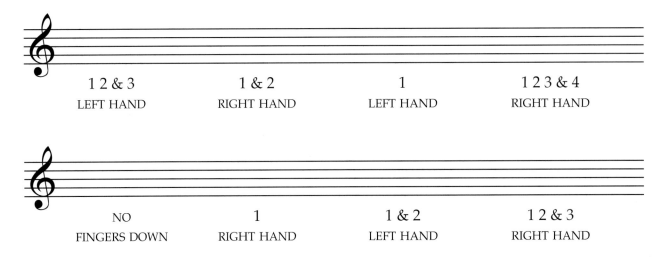

(A reminder: All left-hand fingers down whenever the right hand is operating!)

This is the sort of test you must continually give yourself.

Get a pencil and lightly fill in the correct notes for each fingering – from memory! Then play each note slowly, obeying and memorising the fingering while looking at the note and memorising that too.

When you've tested yourself thoroughly, erase the notes you've written and do it all over again. Then start your routine of practice in a different order. I'll explain. If you read along the lines in a normal way your notes will come out like this:

– not much of a tune, I admit, but good practice, because each note comes as a bit of a surprise. And, if you get too used to an exercise it ceases to be good practice because the concentration begins to wane.

A good rule for practising is – when it begins to sound really good, move on to something else. Practice time should be devoted to things you cannot yet do well – and we all have plenty of them!

Here's a way to vary the routine on even a little exercise like Test One. Try reading downwards instead of sideways so that instead of:

1 ⟶ 2 ⟶ 3 ⟶ 4 ⟶

⟶ 5 ⟶ 6 ⟶ 7 ⟶ 8

you'll be going:

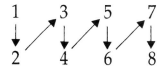

Then the exercise will come out:

When you get too familiar with that, try:

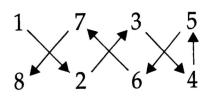

and you'll get:

Apply this principle throughout this book and indeed throughout your studies. Never play scales, arpeggios, or any exercise you will come across later, in the same order every day. The mind gets lazy and one loses concentration. Vary your practice as much as possible. It will sustain your interest and help you to be a better player much more quickly in the long run.

Now, after all those un-tuneful exercises, here are a couple of pieces to make you feel you can make music out of this contraption after all!

THE MOODY BROOD

TIN LIZZY

Interesting Note

The saxophone was invented in about 1841 by Adolphe Sax, a Belgian inventor who made it especially to bridge the gap between the brass and woodwind sections in military bands. It seemed the logical solution – a brass instrument with a woodwind mouthpiece, and its place in the military band was immediately assured. What Sax did not foresee was its frequent use in the symphony orchestra, or of course its later use in jazz, which was not to appear on the music scene until well into the next century.

There is, as far as we know, no monument to Adolphe Sax, or a building or street named after him. But by putting his name to the saxophone he did more to perpetuate it than by any other conceivable method – he added it to the dictionaries of almost every language in the world!

ACT ONE – Session 4
More Notes

18

19

In this next session we are going to learn how to make some more notes. We already have eight at our disposal, but we need a few more to increase our armoury.

The first two new notes are relatively simple to achieve – neither requires the use of different keys, but a different use of the keys we already know.

1. If you put the second finger of your left hand down *(see Figure 18)* (leaving the first finger unused) you will get the sound

C

which is lower than the

C♯

you get with no fingers down but higher than the

B

which comes out when finger 1 is down.

2. Likewise, if you put the second finger of your right hand down, leaving the first finger unused *(See Diagram 19)* (and of course, as always, with all left-hand fingers down) you will get the sound

F♯

which is lower than the

G

you'll get with no right-hand fingers down, but higher than the

F

which comes out when finger 1 is down.

Make yourself familiar with both these new fingerings and practise this new way of going down the notes on the instrument

and then go on to this next exercise which will help you further familiarise yourself with the newcomers –

Now two more new notes. Both of them involve new keys and the first involves a new finger, as we're about to use the fourth (little) finger of the left hand for the first time.

You'll find if you let the 'new' finger fall naturally on to the nearest available key you'll probably find it on the uppermost of a group of keys forming a flat area of metal. (Later this finger will be required to operate this entire group.)

Now that you've located this key, but not depressed it, put fingers 1, 2 and 3 of your left hand down and blow. As we found out in Lesson 3 the sound you'll produce will be

G

Now, while still blowing this note, depress the key under your fourth (little) finger of your left hand *(see Figure 20)*. The note

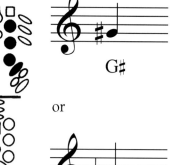

20

G♯

or

A♭

will emerge, which is higher than the note you started blowing, but lower than

A

you would get with just fingers 1 and 2 down.

Now this may be confusing to you. It's the first time we've added to the number of fingers down (from three to four) and got a higher note! Always in the previous lessons, we added fingers to the keys and the notes became lower. (But if you look into a mirror while you perform this latest manoeuvre you'll notice that, unlike all the other keys we've dealt with this far, the latest one doesn't close one of the holes in the instrument – it opens it! And so logic prevails, and our rule of shortening the air-column to get a higher note is still good.)

But keep playing the following, and your fingers will soon acclimatise to the strangeness of the operation.

Don't forget

G♯

and

A♭

are the same (new) note, but written in two different ways. Both ways are included here so that your eye will become used to spotting them at an early stage.

Let's go on to the fourth and last 'new note' in this lesson.

Put the first finger of your left hand on to its allotted key and depress it. Now slide the tip of your finger gently downward about half an inch (1 centimetre) *(see Figure 21)*. You'll come across a small key, smaller than the one you're already depressing, which will lower the note you already had under your finger.

Try this again, only this time blow. You'll hear the note you had at first go lower and the new note

B♭

or

A♯

will come out. It's an important note and your first finger left hand should get used to going to the right place to find it immediately

21

without sliding. To practise this, play this exercise over and over again:

and then

Now that's a lot to take in for one lesson, so don't be despondent if you find it difficult at first. Take the exercises as slowly as you like and speed up later. The important thing is to allow your mind to soak up the new information thoroughly. Here's an exercise which incorporates all the new notes.

– and just to round off a mind-boggling session in a slightly lighter vein, here's a tune to finish with:

Sounds familiar, doesn't it? Only two of the new notes are used in the piece you've just played but, please, go back over this lesson as many times as you need to master it. I promise you won't regret it, because all of these newly introduced notes will crop up from now on very frequently indeed. You'll be so glad you worked on them!

Interesting Note

The pads on a saxophone are very important in that they must cover the holes properly, otherwise there'll be leaks – just as disastrous on a wind instrument as they are in the water system of a house, a car, or in a gas main! Leaks can be caused by warping of the pads by the condensation left in the instrument after use. Get in the habit of swabbing out your sax with a pull-through (which you can get from a good saxophone store). Or even easier (because you can't forget to do it!) is a long mop-like contraption which you can put into the sax when you put it away – and leave it there. It soaks up all the condensation and gives the inside a good 'brush down' whenever you insert it or take it out. But don't forget it's in there, like I once did when demonstrating my soprano sax to an audience of schoolchildren. I blew and nothing came out. When I realised what had happened, and extracted this peculiar thing that looked like a snake in sheep's clothing, the kids roared with laughter. So much so that whenever I've played for children since – I've left it in on purpose!

ACT ONE – Session 5
A Breather

We've been covering a lot of ground over the last two sessions, and it sometimes doesn't pay to proceed too quickly, so this lesson is light on new information on fingering, but heavy on an equally important subject – breathing.

In fact some would say *more* important. Many people, including philosophers and thinkers in some of the world's religions consider breathing as necessary as life itself.

That's not for me to go into in a saxophone tutor, except to say that I truly believe that a study of the art – yes, the art – of breathing is the one most essential factor in the study of any wind instrument.

When I was a very young player I had the privilege of watching and hearing the great American jazz saxophone virtuoso Charlie Parker. I soon began to realise that this great player's breath control was quite extraordinary and that it was somehow linked with his greatness as a musician.

I went back to my home in England and looked for someone who could help me learn to improve my breathing. I found that someone in Phil Parker, an elderly but famous brass teacher in London in the early 'fifties.

In my first session with him he made me stand on a board placed across his 'middle'. He then proceeded to lift me up and down to demonstrate the strength of his breathing action.

He taught me several things about breath control. But two facts stuck in my mind above all the others.

1. It is not correct simply to say you must breathe from the diaphragm. True, the *diaphragm* is used in correct breathing, but it is important to use the *lateral costal* and *upper costal* muscles (located at the bottom and sides of the ribcage respectively) as much as the diaphragm to effect the expansion of the ribcage as well as the lung cavity in order to breathe to full capacity. Which brings us to the second major discovery I made with this extraordinary man.

2. *We do not breathe to expand – we expand to breathe.* This means that we do not take in huge amounts of air to expand our lungs – just the opposite. We operate the muscles round the lung cavity so that the available space expands – and sucks air into the lungs.

The ribcage muscles and the diaphragm together act just like an old-fashioned pair of bellows used to suck in air which could then be expelled to brighten up a dull fire. Think of yourself opening these bellows when you draw in a breath. It'll help you realise how much the control and development of those muscles can increase your capacity for air, not only going into the lungs but, much more important, *going out of the lungs into the saxophone*.

Quality of sound, steadiness of tone, confidence in performance are all greatly affected by the efficiency with which the airstream is sent into your instrument. Don't ever forget that. Do the following without your saxophone.

Stand in front of a mirror. Slowly breathe in to the fullest possible extent, feeling the air get to the very bottom of your lungs and expanding those lower ribs in order to do so.

Then from the *bottom* of the lung cavity gradually expel the air, *first* using the lower ribcage muscles, then *second* the diaphragm, and *third* the upper ribcage muscles, the ones that some singing teachers erroneously advise against using at all. Think of a bicycle pump with its plunger coming from below to force the air out of the chamber into a very small cavity at the top, or the toothpaste tube that I mentioned in Session 2 (page 16).

Do this operation ten times. Each breath should take 20-30 seconds, and by the end of the five minutes you could feel quite dizzy. Don't worry. You've been using parts of your lungs which haven't seen any action for years, and the invigorating effect of oxygen in them is quite overwhelming at first. But in the long run it's very healthy indeed.

Work on your breathing. It's a thing you can do almost any time – when you're walking, sitting still, in a bus or train, driving or even lying in bed trying to get to sleep. In fact, a yawn is often as near to a complete breath as some people ever get. It's as if the body is so starved of oxygen that it switches on a yawn hoping to be invigorated. Next time you yawn notice the way the muscles work.

Now pick up your saxophone. Breathe in by expanding your lung-cavity as I've explained, then as you expel the air from the lungs, do so into the instrument, playing the first note you learned:

C♯

Keep playing the note for as long as you can keep it steady. Time yourself every day and try to improve the endurance. Keep a notebook of your daily timings on all the notes you have learned (the timings will be much better usually on the higher notes than on the lower ones).

Don't forget the newer notes

C   F♯   G♯   B♭

and don't forget to vary the order daily as I mentioned earlier.

As you get used to this routine start listening to yourself. Slowly the 'strained' nature of your sound should be disappearing and a quality tone gradually replacing it. You'll sound better on some notes than others, but the important thing is first to get all the notes you've learned when you want them and, as far as you can tell, reasonably in tune. If you're still experiencing difficulty, maybe you should check the strength of your reed. Try a softer one if you have difficulty holding the notes for as long as I've said you should, or a harder one if your tone is too raucous. Don't forget *low* numbered reed grades are softer, *high* numbers are harder. So if you find a 2^1/$_2$ reed hard to sustain long notes on, try a 2 or a 1^1/$_2$.

But constant experiment and practice will improve your sound, as well as training those muscles around your mouth which make the formation which controls the reed and mouthpiece. It's known as the *embouchure*.

Long notes will help form a good embouchure, but check all the time that your lungs are doing what I've explained they must learn to do. I can assure you that, whether you turn out to be a lifelong saxophone devotee or not, you'll always be thankful that you learned to do what so very few people (amazingly) know how to do properly and efficiently – breathe.

MAKE UP YOUR MIND

Interesting Note

If you're getting really interested in saxophones (and I hope you are) you may be itching for an excuse to go to a music store and nose around a bit.

Well, I've got two excuses. A saxophone is not an easy instrument to 'park'. It's often difficult to find a place to lay it down (apart from the case, which may not be handy) without either risking damage to the finish of the sax or the furniture you've put it on.

The solution is a saxophone stand, which grips the instrument by the bell and holds it upright, ready to grab when you need it again. Sax stands sometimes have pegs on them for accommodating other instruments like flutes or clarinets (in fact a soprano saxophone stand would be a single peg to fit in the bell rather than round it) so that if you already play another instrument it could be useful for that. But if you take sax-playing seriously it could be a good investment for the future.

A sax stand is at this stage admittedly a luxury. My second suggestion for an accessory is in my view an essential part of a musician's equipment – a metronome.

I will not go into the reasons for needing a metronome now. Suffice it to say that later on in this book I will insist you use one in your studies.

Metronomes are usually electronic these days and often have other uses built in besides the main function of measuring and indicating the speed at which music is meant to proceed. Sometimes they will emit notes of correct pitch, which will be handy for you later to check whether you are blowing your instrument in tune. We'll talk about that later when the possibility arises that you may play with other musicians. In the meantime we'll keep our beginner's noises to ourselves!

ACT ONE – Session 6
More Notes

For the last time for a while I'm going to give you more note-fingerings to learn. Just two more. Both of them involve the fourth (or little) fingers, and when you've learned them you've almost completed your required knowledge of the lower notes of the saxophone. So here goes.

The first new note concerns the right hand.

Play the note

D

with fingers 1, 2 and 3 of your right hand down, remembering to keep your left hand fingers down at the same time. Now prepare your fourth finger to go down but instead of leaving it in its usual position pull it upwards to close the gap with the third finger. You'll feel another key there, higher up the instrument but next to your

E

key (*see Figure 22*). Put this key down whilst playing the note

D

and a new note will emerge. On paper it is written as

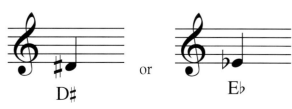

D♯   or   E♭

Play it a few times, moving your little finger up and down

and when you are quite used to the action you will be able to incorporate it into your 'note vocabulary'.

Play this exercise

These two bars should sound the same – they are written differently to keep you alert!

and you'll feel a new thing happening to your fingers. To make the steps which are in brackets, in both cases going up only *one*, you'll be lifting and lowering *three* fingers, 1, 2 and 3. Practise this one a lot, because you must learn to do it fluently and at first it's an illogical-feeling movement. But soon you'll get used to it.

The second new fourth-finger note concerns the left hand. Put fingers 1, 2 and 3 down as if playing the note

G

Then feel for the note

G♯

but instead of playing it move your little finger out and away from the key it was on (and the other fingers). You'll land on the outermost of a little 'plateau' of keys all made for the fourth finger of the left hand (we'll deal with the others in another lesson).

Now play the note

C

without deserting the new position we've found for the left-hand little finger. When the note is established depress this new key (*see Figure 23*). You'll get the sound

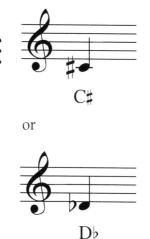

C♯

or

D♭

Once again the movement hardly seems logical to the fingers, but they'll soon learn the job if you keep them working.

A good exercise incorporating both new notes is

23

repeated over and over again. The two bars sound identical, but once again I've written them differently to get you accustomed to the two ways of writing each of the new notes (when you learn more about music notation – if you don't know already – you'll see why the same note is sometimes written in more than one way).

This exercise is also good low note practice. Low notes take a bit more wind and a bit more effort than the higher ones but they are worth it for the lovely sonorous sound they make. And the extra breath shouldn't be a problem if you're taking your breathing seriously. But if they are still proving a bit of a problem in reliability try using a slightly softer reed (or sandpapering or scraping the one you already have to make it softer).

Just to round off this lesson here's a descending passage to play a few times which includes all the more 'tricky' notes you've learned in this session and in Session 4.

The sign ⌢ means that you can pause on the note below it – if you've got any breath left!

Interesting Note

Some simple things get to look very complex. The saxophone mechanism appears a really unfathomable mass of rods and keys. But if you look in a mirror at yourself as you use the 'new' keys and watch for the place on the instrument where the actual 'hole' opens you'll realise that the hole is always in the logical place – higher up the saxophone if the note is higher and lower down if the note is lower in a completely logical way.

If we had about eighteen fingers, and the ends of our fingers were long and the tips as big as potatoes, we could take every key, every rod, and every pad off a saxophone and still play it. We could work the saxophone like a giant recorder, covering the holes with our fingers like a recorder player does. The problems start when we need the lower notes in music. Even a bass recorder starts cheating by having a key on it in addition to all the holes covered by the fingertips, enabling the little finger of the right hand to produce a note from a hole it otherwise couldn't reach.

But the saxophone is unusual in the family of 'reed' and 'woodwind' instruments in having no holes to cover with the fingertips only, with no pads to help. The instruments of the clarinet, oboe and bassoon groups all have, with a few exceptions, open holes to cover manually. And many types of flute as well.

The characteristic sound of the sax is achieved by the large bore, and by the large holes it must have in conjunction with this large bore. So the sax player, for better or for worse, never experiences the 'feel' of actually covering a hole with his fingers to produce a sound.

But there's one big advantage. If you cut your finger by accident you can still wear a large bandage and play, whereas the same cut will reduce your clarinet-playing friends to watching television.

And by this stage, having got this far with your new mission in life, you should feel no temptation to join them! But in case you do, here's a tune that might put a bit of fun back into the proceedings.

SHE'LL BE COMIN' ROUND THE MOUNTAIN

End of Act One

You've reached the end of the first stage of the course, and if you're blowing with some degree of confidence, achieving some sort of quality in the sound you're making, and finding all of the notes you've learned, which are

then you've done pretty well, no matter how slowly or how quickly you've achieved it all. Some students with a knowledge of some other instrument may get to this stage within a couple of weeks (I would suspect a lack of thoroughness if it were anything less) and others with less experience, and less time on their hands perhaps, may go into months. The only thing to be sure of is that you really understand everything that's been mentioned. Go back over it all and check every step, repeating each lesson before you go on to Act Two.

Make another chart like the one in Session 3 of the notes you've learned in Act One, putting the notes in random order. Better still, put each note on a small card

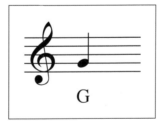

G

D♯

B♭

and so on, then put them in any order and read them off as quickly as is comfortable, say one for each movement of the second hand on a watch, or one for each click of a metronome set at 60 (if you have managed to get hold of one yet).

When you're thoroughly convinced that you've got all you can out of Act One I'll be happy to welcome you to the next phase of your learning experience – Act Two.

ACT TWO

Act One has now been put behind you. In a sense it was the hardest portion of this book because it involves starting from scratch and going through the laborious process of learning the names and the fingerings of many of the notes. And with very little musical reward too – it's difficult to get meaningful or even recognisable music when your knowledge of the instrument is limited.

But all that is going to change in Act Two. More of the hard work, of course, but more rewards too. So stay with it if you've found the going tough, and I promise you some magic moments of achievement before very long.

ACT TWO – Session 7
New Paths

24

Up to now you've learned to play fourteen notes, about 40 per cent of the notes available on most saxophones. Well, you're about to learn the fingerings of another twelve notes – nearly as many again.

If that sounds depressing to you, I've got some good news. The next twelve notes are all virtually identical in fingering to the ones you've already learned!

So here we go. First, play the very first note you ever learned (*see Figure 24*)

C♯

Hold this note, and while still blowing it move your left thumb on to the key near it (which you've so far been avoiding by staying on the thumb rest position).

Press the key, and the note will change to a much higher one *(see Figure 25)*

C♯

25

Then proceed down the instrument, putting each finger down in turn. You'll find that with just the first finger of the left hand, instead of

B

you'll get a higher note:

B

Add the second finger (left hand), and instead of

A

you'll get the higher note

A

Add the third finger (left hand) and instead of

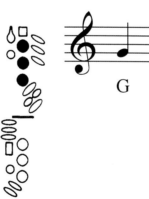

G

you'll get the higher note

G

And then, of course, on to the right hand. Add the first finger (right hand) and instead of

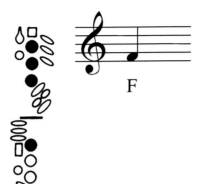

F

you'll get the higher note

F

Add the second finger (right hand) and instead of

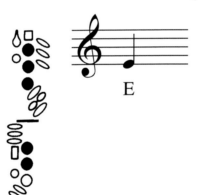

E

you'll get the higher note

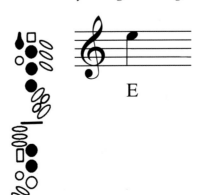

E

Add the third finger (right hand) and instead of

D

you'll get the higher note

D

so that, by the simple addition of the left thumb key (or 'speaker' key, as it's known) you'll get the note an octave higher:

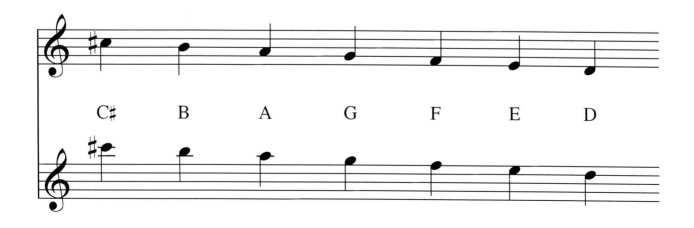

C♯   B   A   G   F   E   D

Likewise, all the other fingerings you've learned within this range are similarly miraculously transformed.

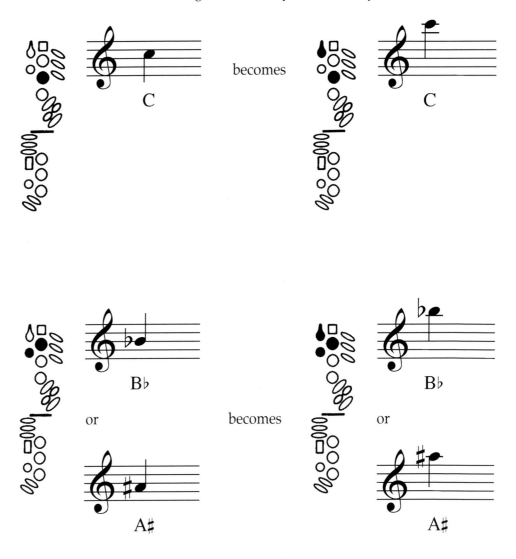

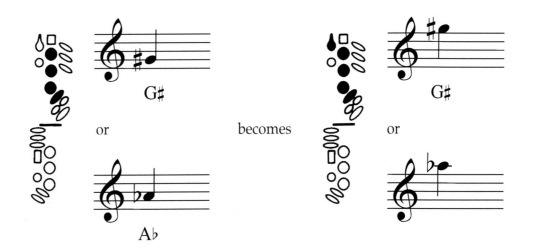

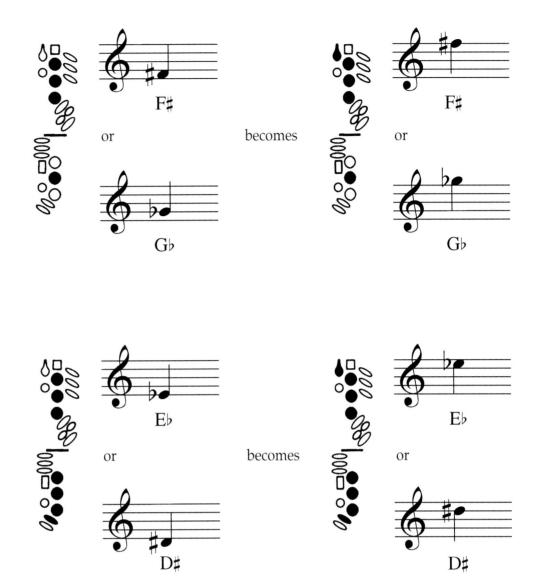

Practise this sequence until you can do it fluently. In future you'll need to be dashing to and fro over it very frequently.

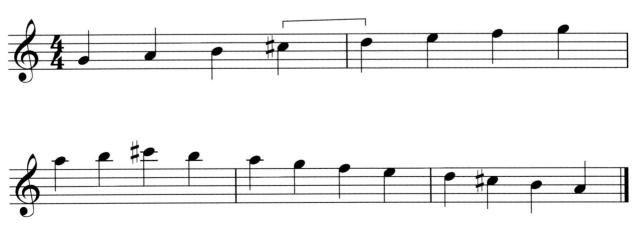

Now seems to be the time for a new practice grid for the *upper octave*, as it's called (meaning all the notes that are made with the help of the thumb-key, sometimes called the octave key).

Do what you did in Session 3 and fill in the new notes which correspond with the old ones (I've done the first one for you as an example). Then go about the grid like a crossword puzzle, across, down, diagonally and in fact in every permutation you can devise.

So even though no new fingerings are involved, there's been plenty to learn in this session. Here's a little relaxation in the form of a tune which you'll recognise if you play it well enough.

Interesting Note

You'll have noticed by now that I am continually placing music in front of you without explaining how it all works. This is because frankly I feel it's too much for a book to do to teach you sax-playing and music notation at the same time. It's better that you get a rough working knowledge of music's written language at this stage, and later concentrate on honing up every aspect of it. The appendix at the back of the book may help answer some of your questions if you are especially curious. But the familiar tunes which I'm using shouldn't pose too many problems, because what you don't know about the writing of them you'll probably be able to guess.

ACT TWO – Session 8
Day by Day

In the last session we introduced the upper octave into our orbit, which will enable us to make great new strides in the discovery of the whole range of the saxophone. Now we are able, or will soon be able, to play 26 notes on the saxophone out of a total of 33 in the usual range of the instrument.

So before we go deeply into this gigantic new land of opportunity it's only right and proper that we should examine a little of what we have achieved so far, and the methods which we have used. Bad habits die hard, and it's best not to acquire them in the first place, and if we do, to stamp them out quickly.

Quite apart from the new material in each session, the student of the saxophone should spend some time on a regular (hopefully daily) routine to maintain and improve the skills he or she is learning. Let's discuss the best way of doing this under the various appropriate headings.

Tone

This is a very important element of saxophone playing. No amount of nimble-fingered playing can disguise a bad tone or make up for it. You must always be conscious of the need to work on it, especially in these early stages of playing. So one daily part of your routine must be

Long note practice

Play every note you know for a count of five seconds (or five beats of a metronome set at 60). Play them at random, varying the pitch as much as possible, for example choosing this sort of sequence

and so on. (This is where an addition to your set of small cards could help (see End of Act One, page 38), increasing them so that you have a card representing every note you know. Then shuffle them and place them in a different order every day.)

Listen to the sounds, and try to find ways of improving them

a. by tightening or loosening the embouchure

b. by taking more or less of the mouthpiece into your mouth

c. by blowing softer or harder

d. by checking your method of breath-expulsion – or

e. by any other way you can discover.

The muscles round your mouth will gradually strengthen and obey your wishes more readily, producing an ever-improving sound. Five minutes a day on tone-production is time well spent.

Scale practice

Music is usually written in what are known as keys. (No relation to the keys on our instrument – this is a completely different use of the word.) There are 14 keys in frequent use, and each one of them uses seven specific notes more than any others.

So it is a good idea (that has worked for centuries) to learn the most-used notes for each key in sets, so that when any one key is about to be used we can be ready for the notes it generally employs. These sets are called scales.

Scales are convenient not only because they inform us of the most important notes for any key, but because they supply us with notes to exercise the fingers, and help the muscles to 'remember' where they should be on a particular occasion.

For example the key of B flat (which is usually written as B♭) uses these notes

I said each scale has seven notes but I've added one more for reasons I'll explain later. Notice that the last note (the eighth) is fingered the same as the first

with the thumb or *octave key* down. Thus we refer to the note

B♭

as being an *octave above* its companion note

B♭

Now play that scale a few times to get the sound and feel of it.

Now here's a tune in the key of B♭. (I've shortened it a bit, but the essence is here.)

THREE BLIND MICE

Check it against the B♭ scale. All the notes are used, so I've proved that playing and getting familiar with the scale of B♭ helps you to play music in that key.

So now will you practise scales for me? They may seem boring at first but they're worth it. And soon I'll be telling you ways of making scales interesting and challenging.

Here's one way to practise scales – first up, and then down

Play this three times, a little faster than one note per second. Set the metronome at about 90 (if you've got one). The last note should last for two beats, however. (Read the Appendix if you don't understand why, or just take my word for it at the moment.)

Here are four more scales to practise:

C three times or more without stopping

G three times at least

F three times or more (at least)

D three times without a mistake (at least)

Don't go too fast at this stage – steadiness and uniformity are much more important than speed. Students who try to break world speed records at this stage usually end up with a rotten sound, so don't be tempted.

Now you'll begin to see the need for good breathing. Sometimes you will find yourself stopping in mid-scale, not because you made a mistake but because your breath ran out! Take a good breath at the start of each exercise, listen and watch your mirror – preferably a big one so that you can see your abdominal muscles as well as your embouchure.

Gradually, if you have a metronome you'll be able to push up the tempo a tiny bit every day to make you think a little faster. But I mean gradually, *very gradually*. Later you'll have fun with scales, in conjunction with a metronome and a stop watch but not now. Your time will come.

Arpeggios

Arpeggios are derived from scales and are continually used in all sorts of music. They are in fact chords, groups of notes which sound harmonious when played all at once on instruments capable of doing this, like the keyboard instruments or the guitar. But they sound almost as good on wind instruments when the notes are played one after the other in sequence.

Here are some simple arpeggios in the five keys we've already got scales for

B♭ three times or more

C three times at least

G three times plus

F   three times (plus several more)

D   until you drop!

So now you're initiated into the world of scales and arpeggios. Keep working on them and in a little while we'll learn how they can be varied and made more interesting.

Experiment time

So now you've done your 'duty work' and are no doubt feeling very noble and self-righteous. Well, all practice sessions should end with some music-making even at this stage of your career.

So you should now have at least ten to fifteen minutes exploring the instrument and finding out things about it that even this book doesn't tell you. Try playing your favourite tune, or play along with the record-player or radio. Pick up a piece of sheet music and see if you can make any sense of the top line. Even if you're baffled at least you've tried.

And if you can't think of anything better, here's a familiar tune to finish with.

WHEN THE SAINTS GO MARCHING IN

If you or your loved ones – or your neighbours –
recognised that then you can't be doing too badly!

SWIRLING

Interesting Note

One of the most common expressions one hears people say about musicians is, 'He's out of tune'. What exactly does that mean?

Western music is usually written and performed in keys, and most instruments are manufactured to perform in those keys before they leave the place of manufacture. However, some instruments, such as pianos, can't be adjusted once they are made (or only with great difficulty) and lots of factors like temperature, humidity and barometric pressure affect the others. The 'fine tuning', the day-by-day adjustment of this second group of instruments is left to the musician.

The solo player will have little trouble over tuning – and that will probably include you at the moment. But from the first note you play as a member of a musical team you'll need to know about tuning.

Hopefully your musical partner or team-mates may be more experienced than you and will advise you as to whether you're in tune. If not, they'll probably say 'you're sharp' or 'you're flat'. As you might then guess, 'sharp' means too high, and 'flat' means too low.

You may remember that at the end of Session 2 I coined the expression 'Longer is lower and shorter is sharper'. So if you are accused of being sharp, and consequently need to make your notes lower (or 'flatter') then you must make your saxophone longer. This you do by pulling the mouthpiece up towards the end of the cork section on the end of the instrument a fraction (a millimetre at the most) and blowing again. This may correct the problem but if not try the same thing again.

And, of course, if the cry is 'you're flat' then you must do just the opposite, and push the mouthpiece further on to the sax. In other words, you are making your sax longer to make the sound lower and shorter to make the sound higher.

ACT TWO – Session 9
The Summit

Your present knowledge of the upper register has been leading you tantalisingly close to the very top notes of the saxophone. So in this lesson we will deal with the remaining upper notes – and get right to the top.

Remember though that in this lesson we are merely learning the fingerings for these notes. The top notes of a saxophone are made to sound good by an experienced player only after a lot of hard work, so don't expect these notes to come immediately under your command. I'll introduce them to your daily routine as gradually as possible.

So here we go.

Take up your playing position with the left thumb operating the octave (speaker) key, and look at the keys on the side of the instrument just above the left hand. The middle one should be quite close to the lower joint of your first finger. Practise pushing it with the lower joint while keeping the octave key down with your thumb at the same time.

Then blow the note

C♯

and press the new key as you've just tried *(see Figure 26)*. You'll get the higher note

D

Practise the new note combined with two others to get used to it by playing

So that's New Note Number One.

Now, without blowing, finger the new note. Then roll your hand slightly upwards and the upper joint of the same first finger should touch or come very near to another side key which looks very like the one you're already using *(see Figure 27)*.

Find a way of depressing it without losing control of the keys you've already got down or of the saxophone as a whole. When you've found a way to do this blow the note

D

and then depress the new key. You'll get the note

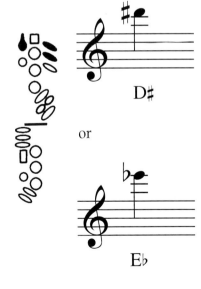

D♯

or

E♭

27

and so acquire New Note Number Two.

If you play this note, and then let your right hand roam upwards on the other side of the instrument (leaving its thumb on the thumb-rest, however) it should eventually come across the uppermost of three side keys *(see Figure 28).*

Press this key down and it will open a hole near the top of the instrument giving the note

28

E

Only one more note to go! Play the last new note which is now keeping both the left and right first fingers busy. But under the lower joint of your left-hand third finger you will find yet another side key lurking *(see Figure 29).* Press it, while keeping all the other keys down (and hanging on with your eyebrows), and with any sort of luck the note

F

will emerge.

29

30

There is one more 'fully fledged' note on many saxophones, the note

F♯

operated by a key on the main body of the instrument near the third finger right hand *(see Figure 30)*. Many saxophones of an older vintage do not have this key, though I'll explain later on how to get this note even if you don't have the special key on your sax.

Now solidify your newly acquired key knowledge by playing this exercise.

Leave out the bracketed notes if your sax doesn't have a high F♯.

The curved line over the top of the notes means you should try to play it smoothly (in one breath, of course) without saying 'ta' (or tonguing) each note.

These new notes will take a little longer to assimilate as the finger movements bear no relationship to the rise and fall of the notes. This applies to most of the new fingerings you'll come across from now on. But you'll be surprised how quickly the mind will accommodate this information, and very shortly your fingers will be moving into these strange positions as soon as your eyes see the note – without you even thinking about it!

But be patient about this or any other step forward in practice. Progress seldom comes quickly. You'll toil away for what seems ages sometimes without any signs of improvement, and then all of a sudden things will fall into place, sometimes when you least expect it.

And don't be worried if you find initial difficulty with reaching and sustaining high notes. Your embouchure is still relatively undeveloped and the muscles are not yet equipped to deal with the problem. Just do the best you can, and in the weeks to come the rest of your practice, particularly your work on long notes and breathing, will gradually make high notes easier to find and sustain, and much more manageable when you get them.

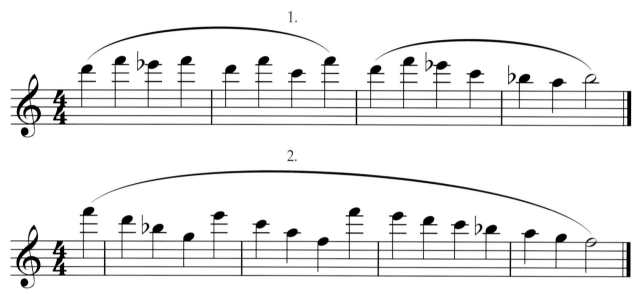

The two exercises I've just written are quite difficult for the beginner. If you find them too hard, come back to them later. But when you can play them well, not only will you feel quite proud of yourself but you'll really be able to start calling yourself a good saxophone player.

Interesting Note

The saxophone was, as you've already read, invented by Adolphe Sax. But he invented not one but twelve saxophones at the same time. There was a series of six – sopranino, soprano, alto, tenor, baritone and bass – giving a choice of six saxes, so to speak. But to make the range even more comprehensive he made another range of 'in-between' sizes so that his range of instruments would suit every need.

The only ones to survive and remain in general use are the soprano, alto, tenor and baritone, all from the first group, and these four (one of each) make a very satisfactory sound when used as a quartet.

One curio remained from the second group for a while, however, and you'll see one around occasionally although they appear to have stopped making it in the 1920s. It's called the C Melody Sax and it filled the gap between the alto and tenor. It seems almost extinct, but then who knows? The soprano almost went out of style at one point yet made a resurgence to its position today as one of the 'big four' saxophones.

ACT TWO – Session 10
Consolidation

Learning the fingerings of the notes and the way they look on paper is of course an essential part of learning the saxophone. But if we surge ahead too quickly we may find ourselves in danger of knowing all about the notes with no real experience of using them; rather like someone with a brand-new car who can show you every feature of it – gear-changing, cruise-control, fog-lamp, and so on – but has only ever learned to drive it round the block. What his driving knowledge needs is experience – a few hundred miles, then a few thousand, then a few hundred thousand to make him a better driver.

But several thousand times round the block won't do it. What he needs to improve is a variety of experiences – driving in busy towns, in mountain passes, on fast motorways, in snow, rain and so forth.

In the same way it's important that we use many different sorts of playing experience to improve our command of the saxophone.

Playing scales helps enormously, but we must vary the type of scale all the time to widen our experience and retain our interest.

Take an ordinary scale over two octaves

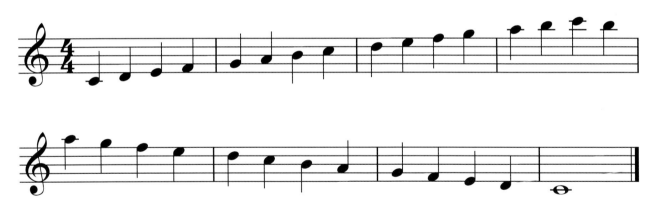

So far we have two options of the way we play that scale. We can either play it smoothly, without using our tongue to separate the notes

etc.

which is indicated in music by the curved line you see over the notes. Or, alternatively, we could play it (as we should if there is no curved line) by 'tonguing' each note (saying 'ta') separately.

ta   ta   ta   ta   ta   ta   ta   ta   ta   ta   ta   etc.

Even with tonguing there is more than one way. A style of playing you'll often come across is playing staccato, which means that almost immediately you make your tongue say 'ta' (and touch and withdraw the tip of your tongue from the reed as you do so) you return your tongue back on to the reed to stop the note. This makes it a very short note! Indeed, that's exactly what is meant by staccato – and a staccato scale means that there should be gaps in between the notes where nothing is heard – silence after every note, in fact.

The sign for notes to be played staccato is dots placed over (or under) them. And so another way to practise scales is

Start slowly at first, then gather speed as you get used to it. Some students have difficulty coping with the lower notes when they first try staccato, so if you do then go back to the earlier exercises in Act One – even to the very first notes and get used to it that way, using 'not-so-low' notes to practise.

Once you've accustomed yourself to the art of staccato, you'll realise that it's possible to play scales using both legato (smooth, un-tongued) and staccato styles

or

and so on. Apply this sort of imagination to your practice whenever you find yourself getting bored or when you think you've mastered a certain scale at a certain speed. The change in the use of the tongue will often reveal faults in your fingering ability which you didn't think were there.

It's often helpful to take a phrase containing a difficulty and repeat it over and over, to give yourself a good dose of the problem, so to speak.

Passages like

or

for instance. It's even better practice not merely to play

but to vary the experience and make it

or even

This can make it a more interesting (though, of course, more difficult) challenge. And it goes without saying that there are almost endless ways to ring the changes on these variations.

Arpeggios too can be treated in this way. For instance, the examples in Session 8 (pages 52-53) can be played

or

to vary them.

Daily improvement

All the variations on the way you practise scales that I've talked about in this chapter are meant to achieve two things – to make you a better player and to keep you interested. In other words to increase your efficiency on the instrument and decrease your feelings of boredom.

This is really important if you want to be a good saxophone player.

It's thrilling to watch a great athlete dash past the winning post or jump an enormous height. But what we don't see at those magic moments is the hundreds of hours of hard, boring training which that athlete has put in to get there.

In the same way, it's a wonderful, exhilarating thing to make good musical sounds on a saxophone – but nobody ever does it without a lot of drudgery. So don't give up when the going is tough – you'll regret it later when you hear someone else play and you say to yourself, 'What an idiot I am. I could have been doing that now, if only I'd kept trying a bit longer.'

We're getting near the end of Act Two, which means that if you've worked thoroughly on everything I've given you, then you must be on the verge of being a player of reasonable ability. And by the end of Act Two you'll know all the notes that are in general use in all saxophone music.

So one last warning. Keep going over the simple exercises in Acts One and Two. Read again the words of advice that you find have been helpful to you – sometimes a sentence or even a phrase can remind you of a very important part of playing as you should. You may have read something like that already – then underline it, or even copy it out and stick it on your bathroom mirror! Or make one up yourself – the art of saxophone playing is something to be taken seriously like a religious scholar or a philosophy student would regard his subject. So have your quotations and texts on the tip of your tongue like *they* often do, and obey them as fervently.

In my early days as a student I found such a phrase in a book of scales and arpeggios. It said something like this. 'In spite of the many enormous and radical changes in the structure of music over the last three hundred years, a thorough study of scales and arpeggios still remains by far the best way – some would say the only way – to master a musical instrument.' I copied that out and stuck it on my bathroom mirror.

Why not put one in the lid of your saxophone case?

Interesting Note

The success of everything you do on the saxophone depends on one factor that we've hardly touched on – your instrument must be working properly.

Now this is not a state of affairs you can ever assume. Only too often I find that instruments that beginners are using are not working properly, and sometimes what is wrong can be corrected in a few minutes – even seconds – once the trouble-spot has been located.

If you feel you've blown the darned thing enough one day, and your lips are sore and your jaw is aching, just stop, lay the instrument down on its side or on its stand – and look at it.

Gaze at the maze of rods, joints, pillions. Feast your eyes on the little holes, pads and keys that seem to have no explanation. Then one by one pick them out and try to figure out how and why they work.

To do this you'll need to operate some of the keys. But by doing this without holding the sax in a playing position you'll gradually begin to understand the mechanism. And what at first looked extremely complicated to you will become more logical to you, and the importance of doing certain things will become apparent.

For instance, the many little cork coverings to the places where one piece of metalwork presses on another are obviously crucial to the working of the instrument. If they are too small, too large, too wide or too narrow they'll cause the key not to go down and the hole we're trying to close will remain open.

Worse still, the cork may drop off altogether causing immediate chaos. But if we know what is wrong we can often fix it, at least so that it will play again until you can get it to an instrument repairman, by replacing the cork with a shaving off a cork from a wine bottle. You can even sometimes buy self-adhesive cork patches from an art supply store or a stationers.

Sometimes an adjustment screw needs a half-turn or so to make a pad cover its hole again as it should. Make sure you have a small set of jewellers' screwdrivers around to do this – they can be bought very cheaply.

And, particularly in the case of the octave key on the crook (the top joint) of the instrument, a little judicious bending can do the trick. When the crook is removed and put in the case it can get bent and will then ruin the operation of the octave key. Look at the way it works carefully, moving the thumb-key as if you were playing it, and bend it as necessary to open and close the little pad on top of the crook correctly. Be careful but don't be afraid. The octave key metal has very rarely been known to snap.

If you suspect a leak somewhere but can't trace it, get someone to press each pad in turn on the instrument with their fingers while you blow a lowish note.

Directly a leak is 'sealed' by the pressure you'll notice the difference in sound and ease of blowing. Then you can find out why it's not working and effect a repair.

Even if you're not too talented at working with cork, glue and screwdrivers yourself, once you know what the problem is you can often enlist the services of someone more practical actually to do the job while you watch.

That's what Tom Sawyer would have done if he'd been a saxophone player. And when he got his horn back he might just have played a tune about trees, like this one.

MULBERRY TREE

ACT TWO – Session 11
Last Notes

You now know how to find every note on the saxophone – except two. And I intend to deal with that straightaway, so that your fingering armoury will be complete, certainly for every eventuality that you'll be encountering in most music. There'll be some new revelations later on to make certain musical passages easier with some more technical knowledge, but you will by the end of this session be able to tackle anything that crops up somehow or other.

The first low note I'll deal with is

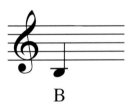

B

and this is found by putting the fourth (little) finger of the left hand on the group of keys which contain the note

G♯

Find this key, then slide your finger (fourth) downwards till it is in command of the key immediately below it *(see Figure 31)*. Then finger and blow the note

C

and afterwards press the new-found key (with your fourth finger left hand, of course) and the lower note

B

will sound. Play the two notes a few times each to get used to it.

31

One more to go. You have already learned now the places in this little cluster of keys for three notes. They are

G♯

C♯

and now

B

But there is one more key there which you so far haven't touched. Find it with your little finger (left hand) and then blow your old friend

C

As soon as you get the note C, push down the key you've just discovered (*see Figure 32*) and the note

B♭

will emerge triumphant.

The reason I'm not so specific about the actual position of this note is because it varies a lot according to the make of instrument. That of course applies a little to some of the other keys, but the instructions and the pictures in

32

this book should be enough to guide you to the right place. The lowest note on the saxophone is dealt with in different ways by different instrument designers and you'll have to live with the particular layout on your instrument.

When you've got used to the feel, you can do some exercises which will give you not only experience in finding your way to other notes from it, but also the strength and control needed to push down those relatively heavy pieces of metal which constitute the bottom notes and the mechanism which controls them.

Here are a couple of phrases which include the sort of problems you may encounter from time to time.

That was relatively easy, but here's a much more tricky one . . .

Don't get too worried if this last one is a problem for you. It's really good practice to work on such phrases, but you'll be relieved to know that the extreme low register of any of the family of saxophones is very rarely encountered in sax music. Even when the low notes are used they are usually found without many movements like the ones in the exercise above. Still, we must be ready for anything in our attempt to tame the saxophone, and all the low-note practice you do will surely pay dividends in improvement in breathing, embouchure and tone. So don't skip this session.

Mousey Fantasy

Interesting Note

You may be surprised to know that now you've learned the fingering system of the saxophone, you've also learned a considerable amount about the clarinet, the flute, the oboe – and even a bit about the bassoon!

You see, even though all these instruments (except the clarinet) have a completely different blowing method from the saxophone, the system of holes in a pipe – opening or closing one by one to make the pipe shorter or longer – works just as well with them as it does with the saxophone.

Indeed, in the world of professional music-making you'll often find saxophone players who are also pretty good on one or more of the other members of the woodwind family. As a matter of fact, you might even be able to get a tune out of a clarinet yourself if you tried, so similar is the system of blowing and fingering. The main difference is that you'd be actually covering notes with some of your fingers instead of pushing down pads to cover those holes (in many cases at any rate).

So if you decide later on to take up another instrument to blow, you'll find that a great amount of the work you've just done to learn saxophone fingering will not have to be repeated.

But please don't go rushing to buy another instrument to study just yet. There's plenty more to learn about the saxophone before you take such a drastic step!

ACT TWO – Session 12
More Practice

We're coming to the end of Act Two – the second phase in your experience of learning to master the saxophone. You now know all the notes, but we are still only going to practise in a few keys. However, we are going to establish a way of working so that we can get the utmost out of the time we are able to devote to our study.

We're going to concentrate on the five basic scales we have already dealt with in Session 8 (page 51). But we are going to start raising our standards, and from now on the scales must be played evenly and rhythmically.

From this point onwards I intend to assume that you've succumbed to my threats and got hold of a metronome. As I've inferred earlier, I feel very strongly that the metronome is practically indispensable for practising an instrument. Its perfect time-keeping will encourage you to play accurately and rhythmically, and it will allow you to measure the improvement in your technique by allowing you to play your scales and arpeggios a little faster each day.

Practice without a metronome is to my mind like trying to lose weight without weighing yourself daily. It becomes so difficult to assess your progress that you're inclined to lose interest.

So let's assume you've got hold of one of these magical instruments. Set the adjustment to 60 and start it. We're going to 'revamp' the scales to make them more suitable to play in strict time, and to keep repeating them for as long as we're able.

The thick double bar-lines with the dots beside them mean that everything in front of them is repeated – that is, played twice instead of once. That's a musical sign which you'll meet in all kinds of music over and over again. However, for our purposes in this book it can often mean 'repeat as many times as you like – or can'. Some of the short phrases you'll meet can be treated like 'tongue-twisters' and you can have fun seeing how many times you can do them without a mistake, pushing up the tempo as you perfect them.

However, back to the scale we've just written. Play it, using *two notes to every beat*. At this speed one 'repeat' will probably be all you can manage comfortably without running out of breath – maybe even no repeats at first. So be it. The important thing to listen (and watch) for is evenness of tone, equal length notes landing at exactly the right place, and correct breathing.

Here's a variation on the simple scale procedure to add spice to your practice. It's called a 'scale in thirds' and uses the same notes as the previous scale in a different order

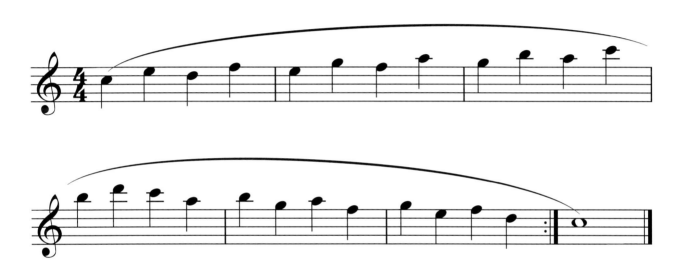

You'll notice that this one is quite a bit longer than the straightforward scale, so it's very unlikely that you'll be able to get through this more than once at the present speed! But later you'll be moving your metronome to speeds more than twice as fast, and then you'll easily tackle it more than once before you settle on the last long note.

When you've satisfied yourself on your performance with these two, both scales in the key of C, go on to the other four scales we're concerned with at the moment, the scales of F, G, B♭ and D. Here they are in the same two forms.

Key of F

Key of F in thirds

Key of G

Key of G in thirds

Key of B♭

Key of B♭ in thirds

Key of D

Key of D in thirds

These are scales over a one octave range. Later we'll extend those scales to cover a larger range, but in the meantime work only on these forms, striving for improvement on speed, rhythm and tone at every speed you set before you move up to a faster tempo.

Interesting Note

You'll notice at the beginning of each scale in this lesson (except the one in C) one or two 'stray' sharps or flats. These little groups are called 'key signatures' and are there in music to remind us that in the key of F, for instance, we'll be encountering one note in each octave with a ♭ sign, or in the key of D there are two notes in each octave with a ♯ sign in front of them.

Try to memorise the number of ♯ (sharps) or ♭ (flats) in every new key you learn about. It will be useful to you later in a way that's difficult to explain fully now. But it's a system that's been in use in Western music for hundreds of years and is still used extensively today. (Students who are already knowledgeable about musical notation from other sources will already be aware of this information, but a reminder can't do any harm.)

End of Act Two

You've now reached a stage where you must be looking to a practice routine. Whether you can afford five hours a day to practise or just ten minutes – a regular system is important.

In Act Three we'll gradually extend the type of practice you should be doing until, frankly, the more time you can spare the more progress you'll make. We'll extend the variety and complexity of scales, to be sure, but we'll also be introducing you to the gentle art of musicianship, which is another subject entirely from the craft of instrumental ability.

Yet you can't have the second without the first! So all the time you've spent so far on the 'drudgery circuit' will be paying dividends in the next and final phase of this book.

So you're in for some enjoyment in Act Three. But don't imagine that the hard work is over – there's plenty of that too! In the meantime, have a shot at this last piece, but don't try dancing to it at the same time.

CAN-CAN

Jacques Offenbach arr. John Dankworth

ACT THREE

This final section of my book will take you a step further in your aim to achieve a good basic technique on the saxophone. I'll be 'rounding off' by dealing with some of the remaining mysteries of the instrument.

By the time you've gone through this last section thoroughly you should have a good enough working knowledge of the saxophone to
1. play and read music for the instrument
2. rehearse and perhaps perform with other musicians.

But what is most important is that you continue to enjoy what you're doing, and that the music, not just the technical progress you've made and will continue to make, gives you increasing pleasure. This last phase will complete your technical armoury to help you to do that.

ACT THREE – Session 13
Daily Routine

Now that you've reached Act Three stage, you'll probably have discovered already how important it is to practise regularly. But now it becomes increasingly important for you to practise not only regularly but *systematically*. This session will help you to do that.

Long notes
Aim – to improve breathing, tone and embouchure control. Metronome setting – 60

EXERCISE ONE
Hold each note for two beats of the metronome.

EXERCISE TWO
Hold each note for three beats of the metronome.

This is a much harder exercise. Do it in front of a mirror and try to get as little variation as possible in embouchure between low and high notes. Don't 'pinch' on the mouthpiece to get the high notes. A good embouchure should produce bottom and top notes with equal ease and virtually no change – always aim for this, even though it may be a long time before you attain anything like perfection.

Even harder is to do this exercise without tonguing each note, but blowing continuously. Even experienced players are apt to sound horrendous attempting that, so try to practise it when there aren't too many listeners! But the benefit to both embouchure and breath-control will be enormous.

At the slow metronome speed you'll have to breathe at intervals throughout this exercise, but at one beat per note you should get a good way through it before collapsing! If you find the beginning with its impossible jumps (the sort admittedly that you'll never meet in real playing, but which are such good practice) too demanding, start on, say, the seventh note.

Spend a genuine five minutes on this one – don't exhaust yourself on it – and then move on.

Scales

A good way to practise scales with a metronome is to play them in a way that they can be easily and rhythmically repeated as often as the breath lasts (and that will, of course, vary with the metronome speed). But scales should always, from now on, cover as much as possible of the range of the instrument, and to do this with every scale we have to plan some differently from others.

The five scales we've already dealt with should now be practised like this:

Scale of C

Scale of F

Scale of G

Scale of D

Scale of B♭

Now that we've reached this stage, I'm adding four more scales in new keys to your daily routine. Here they are in their multi-octave form, using the whole saxophone range.

Scale of E

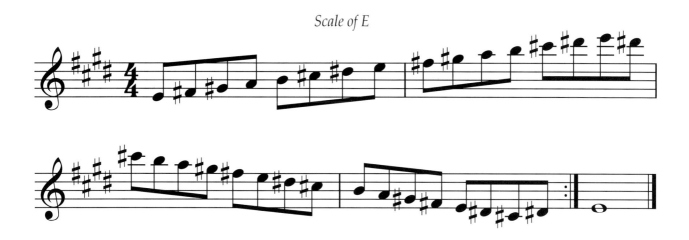

Warning: Now you're getting used to the feel of the scales under your fingers as well as the sound of them, we'll gradually drop the practice of putting the ♯ (sharp) and ♭ (flat) signs in front of each appropriate note as it comes. (The newly introduced ones will continue to have them for a while.) So you must first look at the *key signature* at the beginning of each scale or exercise and remember the drill. In many cases the sound will remind you if you forget.

The only exceptions will come when it's necessary to *cancel* a ♯ or ♭; when, for example, in the key of D an F♯

is not required for the moment, but an ordinary F

is. This is achieved by placing a cancellation sign called a *natural* (♮) in front of the note

telling you to play a straightforward F (and not F♯) for the rest of that bar or measure, in other words until you come to a bar line. Afterwards it automatically reverts to F♯.

There are many ways of using scales to vary practice routine, and I could devote a whole book to them (perhaps I will one day) but here are a few illustrations, which of course can be applied to any key, but are all here in the good old key of C.

Scale in 'recap' C

The above scale can be played with one tongue per bar (as marked above and below the notes), or, much harder, with no tonguing at all. Then the jump from the last note in each bar to the first one of the next becomes a possible problem, especially coming down the scale. But not if you've worked on making your embouchure a good one for all notes high and low, and have been watching yourself in that mirror all the time to check.

Here's another format.

That formation is called a scale in thirds. You can vary
it by altering the order of the notes to go like this

Scales can be treated like this in an almost infinite number of ways –

Scales in fourths

Scales in fifths

Scales in sixths

Scales in eighths – octaves

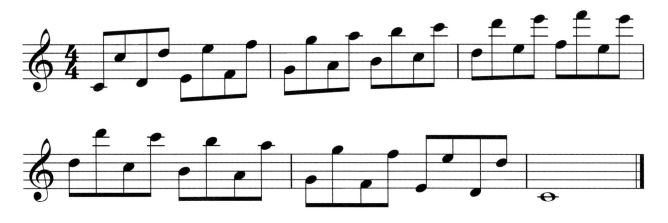

Scales in tenths

– and so on, and so on. If I went on to write them all out (all of them can be played in reverse like the scale in thirds which I began to write in full) it would add zillions of very boring-looking pages to this book.

But now you've reached this stage you can learn a lot – and have a lot of fun working on all these permutations in all the nine keys now available to you, without needing to have them all written down.

Of course, if you'll feel happier having each note in front of you for the moment, then by all means get yourself some manuscript paper and try your hand at writing. If you succeed in putting them all down on paper before your writing hand gives out I give you my personal congratulations.

But the point is to have fun with scales. Keep a notebook of your daily practice, so that you can tell at a glance what forms of scales you've done or not done recently. You might want to give yourself a weekly routine like –

Monday	plain scales
Tuesday	scales in 'recap'
Wednesday	scales in thirds
Thursday	scales in fourths
Friday	scales in fifths
Saturday	scales in octaves
Sunday	scales in tenths

– and each day write down the metronome speed at which you practise each scale (some you may have to take more slowly than others, certainly at first).

Vary the articulation, or tonguing procedure, as much as you can, too. Once again, you could have a day of the week for legato (smooth playing), staccato (short tongued notes) and all the mixtures of the two which you can devise (see page 62, Session 10).

The important thing is to make your scale practice period one which you genuinely look forward to, to keep challenging yourself with things you find difficult, whether those things are whole scales or just four or five notes somewhere in the middle.

If you find yourself sounding too good at a scale, push the metronome tempo up, or alter the articulation to something more tricky. Extend yourself all the time. *Practice in general should not be a time when you're sounding good enough to be congratulating yourself on your progress. If it is, then you, and only you, can very quickly make it harder for yourself so that you're sounding bad enough to realise how much you've still got to learn!*

Interesting Note

You can, of course, treat arpeggios in exactly the same way as scales – invert them, recap them and so on

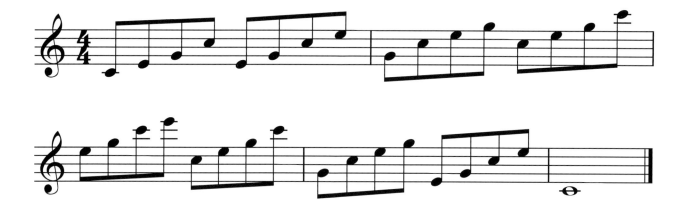

or

with all the tonguing variations as well, of course. Once again variety should be the keynote.

The interesting fact about arpeggios is their name. Arpeggios are in fact chords, and chords are a series of two or more notes which are sounded together. To play chords you either need more than one instrument (one for each note of the chord) or an instrument, like a piano or organ, which will play several notes at the same time. The saxophone is neither, so it has to play each note of a chord one after the other, which can usually give the effect of the chord in question.

Strangely, by tradition this is exactly the way chords are usually played on the harp, not because the harp can't play a number of notes at the same time, but because it sounds better if the notes of the chords are 'spread out'. So Italian composers, when they required a chord to be played in the harpist's style, just wrote on the music the word which said that very clearly – arpeggio or 'like a harp'. This of course applied to all instruments to whom 'broken' or 'spread' chords are now always known as arpeggios.

When you've had your fill of scales and arpeggios for the moment, why not try a bit of ragtime like this piece?

VARSITY RAG

ACT TWO – Session 14
Final Fingerings

There are still a few things about fingerings to know in the basic armoury of the saxophonist which I've not yet dealt with, so after the session entirely devoted to daily practice these new facts may create a pleasant diversion, even a little excitement about pushing out the frontiers even further. Here then is the last round-up.

The long B♭

The notes

B♭

or

A♯

and

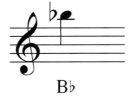

B♭

or

A♯

are easy to get with the fingering you already know. However, passages like

can be made easier by using the 'long' B♭, that is playing the note with the first finger of each hand (without using the small auxiliary key, first finger left hand, which we've associated with the note earlier), or with first finger left hand and second finger right hand *(see Figures 33 and 34).*

33

34

Experiment with the exercise above and you'll see the possible advantages. If you like the feel of it use it in arpeggios too.

The side B♭

Yet another way of playing B♭ in either the lower or upper version is to finger

A   A

and with the inside of your first finger right hand depress the first (or lowest) of those side keys *(see Figure 35)* which we haven't before even mentioned in this book. Once again, this is an alternative fingering, and a little experimentation with it may make you feel its value as an option instead of the other fingering.

35

 or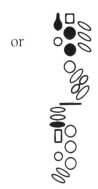

For example,

or

repeated many times very fast would under the present regime all be done with the poor old left hand. By bringing the right hand into use to share the burden by playing the new B♭ we use both hands more or less equally, and divide the workforce, so to speak.

The side C

This is another way of playing

by using the side key immediately above the one we've just dealt with. We finger a

36

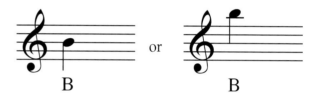

normally and just depress the new key (*see Figure 36*).

Now this key is really much more useful than the side B♭. For instance, you may already have started cursing the fact that every time you change from

you have to move two fingers instead of just one. The side C key will change all that for you. Just try this passage first the old way and then with the side C, and you'll soon be converted. When you're playing scales from now on try to incorporate the new fingerings as well as the old. But in the case of all alternative fingerings keep every option open by practising with them all.

Repeat ad lib.

Articulated G♯

This is a very useful invention which is on most modern saxophones. I hope it's on yours because it makes life so much easier.

Try this. Play the note

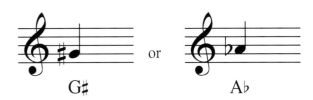

or

G♯   A♭

in the normal way. While still holding the note, press down the second finger right hand, the fingering you'd normally use for

or

F♯   G♭

With most modern saxophones the G♯ will still sound in spite of the fact that you have an 'illegal' finger down – the fourth finger of your left hand. You'll likewise find that you can also finger and play all the right hand notes from

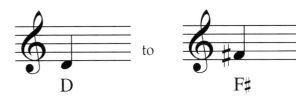

D   to   F♯

in the lower octave and from

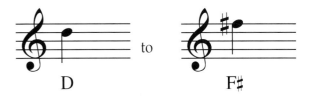

D   to   F♯

in the upper octave.

You'll also find that keeping the little (fourth) finger of your right hand down doesn't affect any of the notes you play with the other fingers of your left hand either (except, of course

Which means that for any scale with the note

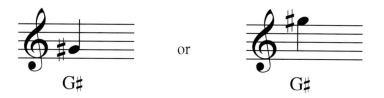

in it (the scales of A and E from the scales we are now using, although B and F♯ will come later on) we can leave that little finger down all the time. Which is very useful in sharp-infested music, if you'll pardon the pun! The articulated

also operates whenever the left-hand fourth finger depresses the

key so that a passage like

– which at any fastish tempo would be somewhere

between difficult and impossible without the articulated G♯ mechanism – becomes very easy with it. Don't forget that the articulated G♯ works in the upper register as well as in the lower one.

Alternative high F and E

Nobody could pretend that one of the highest notes on the saxophone

F

is the most convenient note on the instrument. Its fingering requires that you all but remove both hands from the instrument to get it, and there are times when doing that becomes downright awkward. Fortunately the modern saxophone has another way to do it.
Play the note

C

with the usual fingering (second finger, left hand) leaving the first finger free to roam. Roam upwards a bit and you'll find a button within your reach; press it and – hey presto! – you have your high note *(see Figure 37a)*

37a

F

37b

Hold the note, and put your third finger down in its usual spot (see *Figure 37b*). The magic continues and your

F

becomes an

E

These two notes are of great use in many passages. Without them passages like

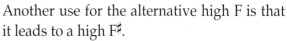

would be a real headache.

Another use for the alternative high F is that it leads to a high F♯.

Play the new F, then use the first finger right hand to depress two notes as shown *(see Figure 37c)*, i.e. normal key plus the B♭ side key we have located and used earlier. A good healthy F♯

37c

F♯

will emerge. What's more, this way of playing

F♯ will work on virtually any saxophone with an alternative top F (the great majority these days).

Many modern saxophones also have a key to use with the right hand, used to go a step higher when playing a high F the *normal* way. Try incorporating one or the other F♯s into your scale practice, especially the scale of D which always sounds to me as if it wants to go to a high F♯!

There is also a lower F♯ or G♭ used in both the octaves in the normal range.

It's only necessary to bother with this one when you've got a fast passage (or trill) going from F to G♭.

Play an F

and depress this new key.

or

You can then leave the first finger right hand down and merely twiddle the new key! Try it for a while – you'll soon get accustomed to it.

TWEEDLEDUM

Well, that's just about it. Until the design department comes up with something new it seems we've covered them all, so all you have to do now is learn them all and have each key and each alternative literally at your fingertips.

On the opposite page is a piece to get you used to the alternative E and F.

Interesting Note

Adolphe Sax, the inventor of the saxophone, was continually working on the creation of new instruments or the improvement of existing ones. His work on the mechanism of the clarinet, for instance, contributed a lot to the sophistication of that important member of the woodwind family, although the work of another designer Theobald Boehm, made even better improvements based on work he had already done on the flute, and thus stole much of Sax's thunder as far as the clarinet is concerned.

Sax did, however, leave one other instrument with his name attached. The Saxhorn is a brass instrument with special characteristics, but it is only occasionally used in the symphony orchestra, usually for music by Richard Strauss.

Still, it's quite an achievement to leave two instruments for posterity with your name attached. Can you think of any others who even supplied one?

ACT THREE – Session 15
Consolidation

Time again for a 'breather', to take stock of the enormous amounts of information we've been taking on board and check to see if there's anything we've not included or worked on sufficiently.

Expression marks

There are many ways for composers to give the musician some idea of the feeling intended to be conveyed by the music they have written. They can often put just one word at the top of the piece, like 'sadly' or 'jauntily' (sometimes they will write them in Italian, the musician's language, which is understood worldwide – then it would be 'triste' or 'giocoso' instead) and we can immediately get a good idea of how to play the piece. And the speed can easily be indicated by giving us a metronome indication too

(like ($\mathbf{\downarrow} = 100$) or ($\mathbf{\downarrow.} = 80$)).

But by far the most common marking any composer makes is the one which tells a player to play loud or soft, or to get progressively louder and softer.
Louds and softs are easy.

$\boldsymbol{f}$ stands for *forte* (Italian for loud) and the more 'fs' you see, the louder you play.

$\boldsymbol{p}$ stands for *piano* (Italian for soft) and the more 'ps' you see, the softer you play.

$\boldsymbol{mp}$ or $\boldsymbol{mf}$ (m stands for *mezzo*)

means 'moderately soft/loud', a sort of 'no-man's land'.

Getting louder or softer

There's an Italian word for each of these too:
Crescendo (usually shortened to *cresc.*) for getting louder or *diminuendo* (or *dim.*) for getting softer.
But there's another way to indicate these. You can use the signs

———————   and   ———————   instead.

And so you'll see there's a *huge* difference between these four pieces of music.

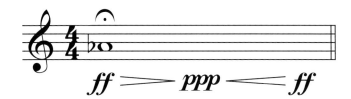

Now the composer in each of those cases may well have written those instructions (we call them *dynamics*) to convey the deep feelings to be conveyed in the whole musical picture being 'painted'. In other words, the dynamics come from the heart.

And do you know where we have to deal with them? *From the stomach!*

Well, that shouldn't come as too much of a surprise, because I did emphasise very early in this book

a.   how important breath control was to all aspects of playing and

b.   I explained how big a part the abdomen plays in breathing.

So, even if the word 'stomach' is not quite biologically right, you get the meaning, I'm sure.

I explained earlier (Session 2, page 16) how the air inhaled into the lungs should be expelled, like toothpaste from a tube or dispenser, from the bottom up, using the muscles of the abdomen first, and later the side muscles around the base of the rib-cage.

Well, this is not only the whole motive power of sax-playing, but the whole art of expression depends on the *speed* at which the air is forced into the instrument. Therefore, when the eye sees

it transmits to the brain the required message which is of course 'get louder and then get softer'. The brain then tells the stomach and the other muscles 'push slowly, then gradually push harder and then back to slow again'.

So from now on all long-note practice should include dynamics. Don't neglect them. It's easy, for instance, to play

but not all easy to play

So that's one more thing to complicate your life, and make sure you don't forge ahead too fast, or, what is worse, get complacent.

Embouchure

You must also be watching (don't forget that mirror) and checking your embouchure, and listening for the sound you're coaxing from the instrument.

It's possible that you may be having trouble with high or low notes – or both. If so, now's the time to check your method of placing the instrument in your mouth. And watch for signs of straining and pinching on high notes.

As you build the muscles around your mouth you will have less trouble with high notes, as those muscles will automatically do the right thing to attain them. If you spot your neck tightening (which tends to close your throat and impede the airstream) or you feel yourself biting on the mouthpiece, you're not blowing correctly.

But, above all, don't despair if you're not getting the sound you want from part of the instrument – or even if you're not getting anything at all. I often encounter otherwise good players who have a 'hang-up' on this part of playing, but so far they've all got over it. But it's sometimes a hard period where you must keep experimenting until the great breakthrough comes – and come it always does.

Finger technique

The scales you are practising daily with ever-increasing fanatical fervour (I hope!) must now be doing your finger technique a great deal of good.

But be careful here. Don't just thunder up and down the scales aimlessly. Directly you find it is coming easily listen to your scales carefully as you play them – always to a metronome, I hope. Don't be satisfied if any tiny segment of the scale gets just ahead or just behind the beat – do it again.

Think of your fingers as hitting tiny drums instead of keys on the downward scales, and of your finger*nails* hitting imaginary drums suspended about half an inch (1cm) above them. And directly you *are* reasonably satisfied with your progress for that day, move on to a faster tempo of the same scale, or to a different one.

Don't forget, once you sound good on any particular part of your practice routine you're on the verge of wasting time.

Tonguing

And lastly, for the moment anyway, make sure your tongue is keeping up with your fingers, your lungs and your brain in this quest for saxophone supremacy. It's not enough merely to be able to move your tongue in rapid succession. You must be able to use it in conjunction with the fingers in all situations. You may find that you can work up a tidy metronome speed on a staccato scale in the key of C. Then switch immediately to the key of, say, A♭. You quite possibly won't make the pace. Tonguing a scale, especially staccato, makes it necessary for the fingers to move much quicker than with a non-tongued scale.

And, of course, mixtures of staccato and legato phrasing can make things even harder. A section of a scale like

played reasonably fast can pose its problems for a beginner, but

or

can pose quite another set of problems, but make the section sound really good.

So bear all these pearls of wisdom in mind as you practise, and get even more benefit out of those precious hours (or parts of an hour) which you devote to your saxophone. Adolphe (Sax, of course) would be justly proud of you.

LONGBOATS

Interesting Note

All three aspects of the physical part of sax-playing can be practised *away* from the instrument.

Breathing can be practised almost anywhere – sitting in a train or bus, standing in a subway or at a bus-stop, or even while driving. But be careful if you are in charge of a car – correct breathing, when you're not accustomed to it, can make you feel a bit dizzy.

Finger technique is another thing you can do anywhere. Think of a phrase which you continually have trouble with – a real 'finger-twister' and rehearse it on your knee or on a table top or an umbrella. (Of course, if you do have your instrument, but noise is a problem, you can do all sorts of scale and arpeggio practice without blowing.)

Tonguing and embouchure can be practised almost anywhere, and, of course, it's always possible to slip your mouthpiece (complete with reed, ligature and mouthpiece cover) in your pocket or bag and practise whenever you have a private moment.

So, unfortunately, I won't accept absence from your instrument, or the neighbours' objections, as an excuse for no practice. Practise something wherever and whenever you can.

If you do so you'll prove your true dedication, because however careful you are you'll find yourself fingering away in mid-air, or grimacing frighteningly as you practise your embouchure – and you'll be getting some very strange looks from time to time from alarmed passers-by. And if somehow they find out you have anything to do with music they'll probably go away saying, 'I knew it, musicians are all crazy'.

And I think I'd probably agree with that!

ACT THREE – Session 16
Final Scales

You already know nine of the fourteen generally available scales, and hopefully you're very familiar with them by now. So here are the remaining ones to complete the set.

Scale of D♭

Scale of B

Scale of G♭

Scale of F♯

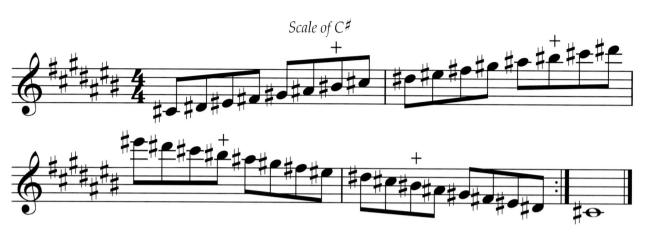

Scale of C♯

There are a few mysteries to clear up here, as you've probably noticed. First of all, the notes marked * and + are new to you, and present a problem if you're not familiar with musical notation. Here's how it works:

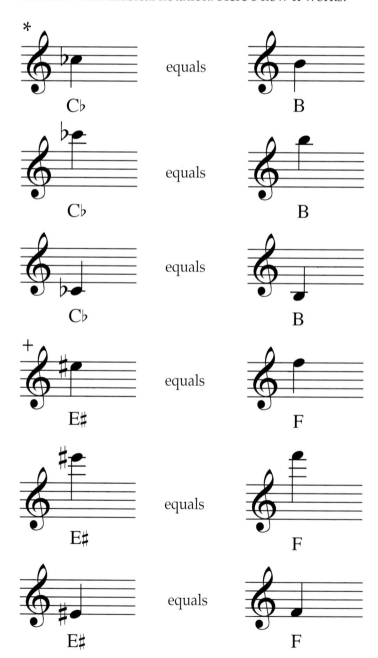

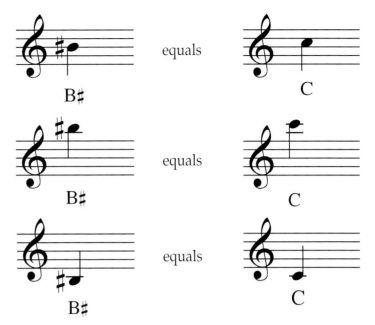

What a complication you may think! It certainly seems a strange thing to do – but then many of the other notes you've learned have more than one way of being written, so these shouldn't come as too much of a shock. The reasons for multiple naming of notes will become apparent to you as you get further into musical notation. The important thing is that your eye gets to recognise every alternative for the same note quickly, and your fingers learn to find it immediately.

The other thing you may have noticed about the scales is that while the scales of F♯ and G♭, C♯ and D♭ look very different, *they sound identical*. So why practise the same scale twice?

The answer is that *looking* at the two scales reinforces your ability to recognise notes and play them *at sight*.

Sight-reading is one of the most important assets to a musician. Many musicians who are not creatively gifted are nevertheless in great demand because of their ability to make written music sound good quickly. In the music profession time is money, and results have to be produced rapidly to minimise cost.

But even in amateur music circles the musicians who are invited to take part in the most interesting musical events are the good readers.

Even in the jazz world, where improvisation is used a great deal, and the ability to play without music is sometimes important, good sight-reading is nevertheless a tremendous asset. And while in bygone years *some* of the jazz 'greats' were poor readers, others were excellent all-round musicians. And of the jazz virtuosi of the present day, virtually all are capable sight-readers, and have a background of thorough musicianship.

And don't forget, of course, that good sight-reading doesn't refer only to the notes. The eye must take in all the expression marks on the page, as well as all the written instructions regarding cuts, repeats and so on. So all in all, you just *can't* have too much practice in sight-reading.

There are plenty more scales to learn later on in the study of any instrument – hundreds, in fact – and these can wait until at least the next phase of our studies. But one particular style of scale shouldn't be postponed that long because

a.   it's a very beneficial scale to practise, and

b.   because we keep meeting bits of it in almost every kind of music.

It's called the *chromatic* scale, and the reason why it's good for practice is that it can encompass every single note on the saxophone.

Try this

Note: ♮ means that any sharp or flat on that note is cancelled.

Practise the chromatic scale slowly at first (if you find it exhausting to start on the bottom note, try starting on the fifth one) and gradually work up speed until you can do it all in one breath – if you can manage a repeat you're really getting on like the proverbial house on fire!

But once again remember to keep strictly in time with your metronome, however fast you're able to manage the exercise. Chromatic scales are very tempting to buzz up and down as fast as you can manage, but you must practise them rhythmically to get the best out of your practice.

One more reminder about the scales you've just learned – use the articulated G♮ (see Session 14, page 95). In the scale of D♭, for instance, after you've played the first note keep the little (fourth) finger left hand down, and go on and play the next four notes. The fifth note will come out

A♭

even though your little finger is still on the key for the first note *and not even touching* the key we have learned for the note! And there you can leave it throughout the whole scale.

And in the scale of B, after you slide your little finger from the first note to the second

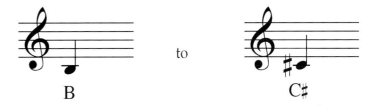

B   to   C♯

leave it down on the second note and proceed with the scale in exactly the same way.

The method takes a lot of the difficulty out of scale-playing in the harder keys and will greatly help to speed up your performance when necessary.

This may seem a short lesson on paper, but there's plenty to practise here. So don't rush it – first take a few minutes off from scales and play this study which uses just an occasional scale to help it along.

PRESSED 'O'

Interesting Note

One of the best-known saxophone solos in the symphonic world is the *Rhapsody for Alto Sax* by Claude Debussy. The writing of it came about as a result of a chance meeting in Europe between Debussy and an American lady who was president of a music society. She persuaded Debussy to write such a piece, paying him a down-payment on the commissioning fee on the spot.

Some time later she wrote to him, asking about the progress of the work, about which Debussy had apparently forgotten.

He responded by asking for the rest of his money, on receipt of which he would send the completed score. This all duly happened, and the world was the richer by another masterpiece from the famous composer.

Such is the power of money!

ACT THREE – Session 17
Mostly for Later

The information in this last-but-one session is somewhat advanced stuff for someone as close to the beginning of his/her saxophone career as yourself.

But I felt it worthwhile to tell you a little bit about things in store for you if you ever intend to take your studies on to a more advanced level. So here are a few things to mull over.

The upper reaches

The low notes of a saxophone are there and there's little or nothing we can do to go lower (but see Interesting Note at the end of this lesson).

However, the upper end of a saxophone's range is limited only by the skill of the player.

Here are some of the fingerings for notes even higher than the range which is dealt with by the keys.

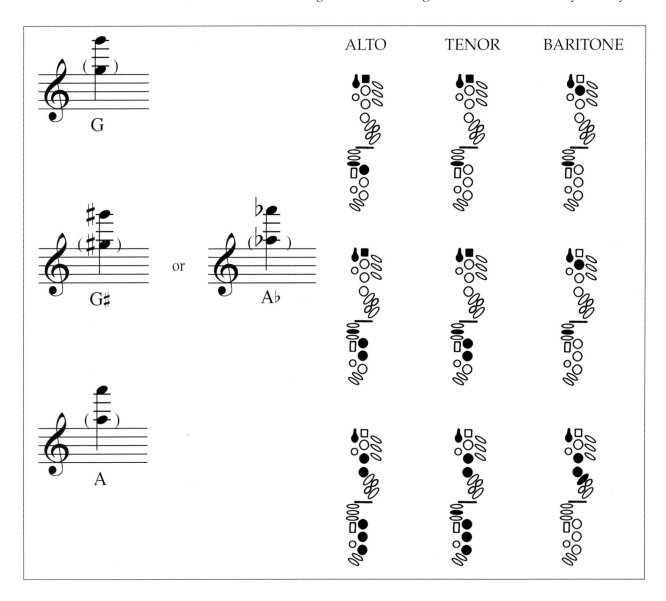

Special thanks to Tim Garland (tenor) and John Williams (baritone), two of Britain's foremost exponents of their instruments, for supplying harmonic fingerings relating to their own instruments for this chart.

Be warned! Harmonic fingerings vary considerably with each individual instrument; thus the above should be taken only as a guide, and perhaps an aid to experimentation. If a fingering does not work for you, try the same note from the other two charts – many fingerings resemble each other closely across the saxophone family.

To play these notes, called *harmonics*, it is important to 'hear' in your head the note you're aiming for. If you play the note in brackets underneath the uppermost note, you'll be in fact playing the note you're after in a different *octave* – an *octave below*, in fact. This should help you imagine the note you're actually trying to get.

Don't take harmonics too seriously at present – there's plenty of work to be done with the more conventional notes on the instrument – but they'll provide an occasional diversion from an overdose of practice!

Circular breathing

The trouble with breathing is that it has to stop sooner or later. You have to stop blowing air out of your lungs in order to take more in.

That's true, and will forever be so. But you *can* continue to blow a saxophone without stopping for breath!

How is it done? By breathing in through the nostrils to the lungs, and at the same time keeping the air flowing into the instrument by using the mouth as a bellows to act as a temporary substitute for the lungs. It's a very useful 'trick' which can be of very practical use from time to time, and it's worth developing. Like most things that come hard at first – from riding a bicycle onwards – it's a question of acquiring a 'knack'.

Try blowing bubbles in a glass of water through a drinking straw. Once you've got things going squeeze your cheeks together. You'll find the airstream is sustained by this action, and that you can actually stop exhaling. You can practise the 'cheek squeeze' away from the drinking glass at any spare moment. Just try to make a wheezing noise through your closed lips by making your cheeks do the work of bellows.

Once you've got the knack of activating your cheeks in this way, the act of inhaling through your nose at the same time will come easily if you keep at it. And then gradually – on notes in the middle range only at first – it will come, I promise you. Australian aborigines have been circular-breathing for centuries on the *didgeridoo*, one of their national instruments. And glass-blowers have done it for almost the same amount of time in the Western world. So it really shouldn't be beyond you, should it? But don't worry if it won't come at the moment. It's not an essential – in fact the majority of woodwind and brass players go through their whole careers without being able to master circular-breathing.

Transposing

This is a subsidiary of the noble art of sight-reading. It means reading a piece in one key and playing it in another. It's a skill you *may* not be called upon to use for months or even years at a time, but when you *do* get asked to do it, you can impress people no end if you transpose well.

As a variant to scales, arpeggios and studies it makes a nice change to try transposing at sight. Have a go at any of the exercises you've encountered in the book. Even scales or arpeggios. Put everything up a tone so that

sounds

or any other interval you fancy. In simple music your ear should tell you how correct or incorrect you are. Once again, the time spent on this chore may well pay off handsomely sometime in the future when for some unforeseen reason everyone in the orchestra is required to transpose – and you've practised it and they haven't.

Interesting Note

Although in general all saxophones go to the lowest note

B♭

the baritone sax is sometimes fitted with an

A

This is an extremely useful note to have as the baritone is often expected to play in unison with other instruments whose range *does* include this note.

Anyway I wrote a score once requiring a bottom 'A' and was expecting a baritone sax player who could cope with it. He was ill and sent a deputy who had no bottom 'A' on his instrument.

So when we came to the recording I found that in the few bars rest I had before the end, I had time to pick up a piece of cardboard and half cover the bell of the baritone sax, which made the bottom B♭ into an A – a rather unorthodox way of doing it, but nobody outside the recording studio ever suspected a thing.

And there's a musical lesson to learn there. The means is not important – it's the end product that counts.

ACT THREE – Session 18
Final Advice

Here we are at the last session.

Perhaps you had thought at times you'd never get here, but you've persevered with all the many difficulties that assail the budding player.

Of course, this isn't the end, but only the end of the beginning – if you see what I mean. You've still got many, many hours of work at that tone of yours, your breath control, your finger technique and your reading and interpretation. Keep doing your practice *regularly* (don't forget that half an hour six days a week is twice as beneficial as three hours once a week) and *don't depart from my recommended methods*. Some of my major points you should know so well by now that you'll groan when I mention them yet again. But here they are just once more.

Rules for practice

1. Always use a metronome.
2. Always watch yourself in a mirror.
3. Always *read* your scales and arpeggios and look at every note.
4. Don't neglect breathing exercises in the pursuit of finger technique.
5. Concentrate most of your practice on things you can't do, not on things you can do. It's dangerous to sound too good when you're practising.
6. Vary your practice routine constantly – use the *card system* to make sure you do all scales and arpeggios at random.

Of course there's more to it than that, otherwise there'd have been no need for all the other thousands of words I've written here to help you. But those six salient points are worth writing a hundred times if it means getting the message home.

Playing by ear

I've emphasised that you must look at the notes you're playing all the time, so that the written note gets engraved on your mind as you finger each note. This is so very important to make you a good sight-reader. But having said that, I nevertheless recommend that you spend some time on your instrument *playing without music*.

Every musician should strive to become not just a pusher of buttons to produce notes, but someone who can use his intelligence to interpret written music and bring it to life. And he can only do that by *listening* to the sounds that he produces.

Far too many budding players manage to get the notes that are on paper, but pay no attention to the *effect* those notes are creating. By playing without music you train yourself to listen only to the sounds you are making. And by finding your own way up and down your instrument, picking out a few notes of a tune perhaps, or just making one up, you improve the sharpness of your ear – and you free yourself from the tyranny of the printed note! Saxophonists of the world unite!

Seriously, though, throughout the world there are thousands of sax-players brought up to read music who deeply envy someone who can play by ear, and thousands of others do without music who wish they were better sight-readers.

So why not be both?

That's *my* ambition for you anyway. Every generation brings a larger crop of musicians who can play highly disciplined written music *and* can also play without music and improvise skilfully. They're the shining examples who show that it *can* be done.

You might be in that special category of someone who can be brilliant on both sides of that music fence, so to speak – or you may not. But in either case you can do your playing and your enjoyment of music a world of good by keeping your musical perspectives as broad as possible in the following ways.

Listen to music as often as you can – music of all sorts. Not just saxophone music either (although you'll soon get pretty good at picking out the sound of a saxophone if it's there). It can be classical, jazz, rock, flamenco, Armenian music, early music, Indian classical music – it matters not a jot, if you do one thing all the time, and that is *analyse*.

Try to figure out exactly what every instrument is doing, try to remember something of the melody (if it has any melody), try to imagine yourself playing along with it. Listen, digest and learn a lesson on the effect of music every time you hear any. You may not like it all, needless to say, but we can always learn valuable lessons on what *not* to do as well as the other way round.

The one thing I can't give you in this book is contact with other musicians. Contact is important, so that problems can be compared and discussed. So to compensate for this you must use every opportunity to talk to musicians – saxophone-players if possible – and learn from them. Next time you hear live music and see a sax-player, make a point of striking up a conversation with him. He or she may be a student of comparable ability, or maybe a world-famous virtuoso. Either way you should go and chat and pick up some information. You may get an occasional rebuff, but don't be put off. To balance that, from time to time you'll find someone who is very communicative and will help you on your way more than you ever believed possible.

And, of course, even though I'm delighted that you've used this book to get you this far, I must admit that instruction books can never entirely take the place of a human being, try as we might to make them do so. So if you're able to find a *good* player or teacher in your area, try to arrange a meeting or even a lesson or two. Now that you have got to a reasonable stage of competence you'll be much more likely to be taken on by a good teacher than if you were a beginner.

And there's another reason. I obviously think the methods I've used here are good ones and believe the information I've given to be the correct method of going about saxophone self-tuition. But there's always room for a second opinion and, who knows, if you still have 'hang-ups' about certain aspects of your playing (and I still do after all my years of it!) a personal teacher may be able to detect and correct something in a way that I couldn't, with our 'remote control' teacher-student relationship!

The only thing that matters is that you continue to improve, and continue to feel part of that international élite – the family of the saxophone. There's a whole world of people out there who have dedicated themselves to this fascinating instrument, and lots of happy times waiting for anyone who cares to join them!

And so here, student, we part. It's been an enjoyable journey together – at least I can honestly say that it has been for me – and I wish you many, many hours, days, weeks and years of blissful music-making.

Or as Adolphe Sax might have said – 'Bon voyage et bonne chance!'

APPENDIX
Musical Notation

*This is a basic introduction to **some** of the rudiments of music. It should be sufficient for users of this book, but it is far from complete. I advise you to further your knowledge by acquiring one of the many books available on the subject.*

Musical notation is a system of putting on to paper a group of signs which tell us how to play (or sing) a given piece of music.

The first things we need to know about a piece are its *metre* (the number of beats in each bar) and its *speed* (the number of beats per minute).

Metre

The metre is put on paper in the form of bars or measures. The composer normally decides what form this should take, but even in folk music with no known composer the metre has to be identified before it can be written down. Usually the natural way we want to tap our feet to music indicates the bar lengths (we tend to tap once or perhaps twice a bar – in waltz time it is almost invariably once). So bar-lines normally come at either every 'foot-tap' or every other one.

Speed

This is often indicated by Italian words like *Presto* (very fast), *Allegro* (fastish), *Moderato* (easy-going), *Andante* (even easier-going!), *Largo* (slow) and *Lento* (very slow). But often words in English are used, making life much easier.

A more accurate method is to indicate the number of beats per minute the piece deals with at the correct tempo. A marking (♩ = 60) would indicate that 60 beats are performed in one minute. (The second hand on a watch or clock, by the way, ticks at 60 beats per minute – obvious, I suppose, but it sometimes surprises people when put that way.) Likewise, a marking (♩ = 100) would mean, if the music contained four beats to every bar, that 25 bars would be performed in one minute, i.e. a medium slow tempo. A *metronome* (ticking machine) will tick for you at *any* given number of beats per minute.

This gives us general information about some aspects of deciphering musical code. But of course we need information about every note of a piece in order to perform it.

The fine-tune details of each note we need to know are basically (a) the *pitch* and (b) the *duration*.

Pitch

The pitch of a note is indicated by its position on, over or below a system of five lines called a *stave*. For sax players the lines and spaces are always designated as below:

Lines

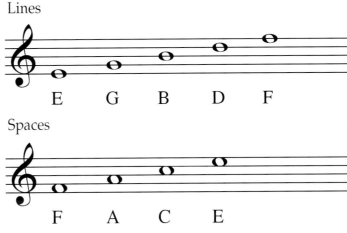

E   G   B   D   F

Spaces

F   A   C   E

Above and below the stave the naming proceeds logically, i.e.:

D   C   B   G   A   B   C   D   E   F   G

The pitch of notes can be altered temporarily by sharps (♯), flats (♭) and naturals (♮). These symbols are placed directly in front of the note they affect, and the change applies to all repetitions of that note for the rest of the bar, after which the note reverts to its original pitch. These occasional amendments are called *accidentals*. The pitch of notes can be altered more permanently by *key signatures*, e.g.

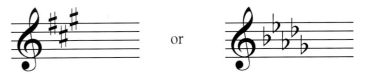   or

Key signatures alter the pitch of *all* notes in the music which bear the names of the lines or spaces on which the key signature lies. The 'command' of the key signature can be changed by single 'accidentals' inserted in the music, but such changes last only for the bar in which they are introduced.

Duration

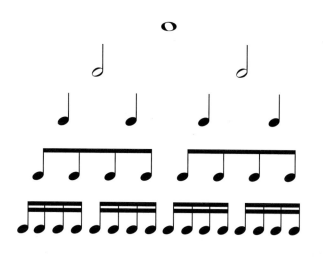

Semibreve (Whole note) = 4 beats

Minim (Half note) = 2 beats

Crotchet (Quarter note) = 1 beat

Quaver (Eighth note) = 1/2 beat

Semiquaver (Sixteenth note) = 1/4 beat

A dot placed after a note increases its length by half

'Tied' notes are played for a total of their combined length without a break

The tails of notes are sometimes written separately

instead of

Time signatures and bar divisions

Time signatures indicate the number of beats in a bar (top figure) and the type of note (bottom figure), e.g.

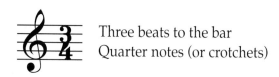

Three beats to the bar
Quarter notes (or crotchets)

A bar or measure is a unit of music which indicates its metre or pulse. It is written as a vertical line dividing equal portions of the stave, making it easier to read the notes and consequently to make sense of the music.

The most common bar lengths are:

Two ♩ beats in a bar

Three ♩ beats in a bar

Four ♩ beats in a bar

Two ♩. beats in a bar

Four ♩. beats in a bar

Other signs and instructions

= *crescendo (cresc.)*   =   get gradually louder

= *diminuendo (dim.)*   =   get gradually softer

rallentando (rall.)   =   slow down gradually

p   =   quiet

pp   =   very quiet

f   =   loud

ff   =   very loud

mp   =   moderately quiet

mf   =   moderately loud

⌒   =   an indefinite pause

=   Repeat the passage in between the thick bar-lines with dots

JOHN DANKWORTH

Born into a musical family in London in 1927, John began violin and piano lessons at an early age. But it was hearing a Benny Goodman record at the age of sixteen which led him to take up the clarinet. At seventeen he entered the Royal Academy of Music, and that was followed by a spell in the army.

It was the inspiration of John Hodges which made him turn to the alto saxophone and this interest was reinforced by his admiration for the great Charlie Parker with whom he played at the Paris Jazz Festival in 1949. At that time John was voted Britain's Musician of the Year and his career as a jazz musician was well on its way. In 1950 he started a small group known as the Dankworth Seven which became a successful vehicle not only for his ability on the alto sax, but also for his skills as a composer and arranger, as well as being a showcase for several aspiring and talented jazz musicians of the day.

In 1953 he moved on to found a large jazz orchestra or 'big band' which was soon earning the applause of both public and critics alike. His band made popular records, including two big hits – *Experiments with Mice* and *African Waltz* – and in 1959 was invited to the Newport Jazz Festival. This was followed by concert performances in New York, sharing the bill with the Duke Ellington Orchestra and at one point being joined by Louis Armstrong. This was only the first of many successful visits to the United States.

John's big band attracted many respected jazz soloists both on stage and in recordings, and his lead singer, Cleo Laine, who became his wife in 1958, established herself as one of Britain's best known female jazz vocalists. Frequent live concerts and radio shows in this period included performances with such legendary figures as Nat 'King' Cole and Ella Fitzgerald. In fact, the list of world-renowned jazz artists with whom John has performed over the years is almost endless and is evidence not only of his musical talent but also of his life-long energetic involvement at the very centre of the international jazz scene.

It was in the 'sixties that John became involved with the film industry, working on scores for films such as *Saturday Night and Sunday Morning* and *Modesty Blaise* and alongside directors such as Peter Hall and John Schlesinger. He has also written music for the National Theatre and the Royal Shakespeare Company, as well as two musicals, an opera/ballet, a piano concerto, a string quartet, several works for choir and orchestra, and a set of symphonic variations for the Royal Philharmonic Orchestra. In 1985 he founded the London Symphony Orchestra's Summer Pops and has conducted many other symphony orchestras throughout the world – all of which bears witness to the genuine breadth of his musical interests and his desire to break down barriers between the various musical factions.

One of his particular concerns and achievements has been in the field of musical education – the encouragement of others, not least young musicians, to practise and develop their skills. In 1970 he and his wife founded 'The Stables', a music centre in the grounds of their home, which has become the base for masterclasses, residential courses, children's summer music camps and about 150 concerts every year, and continues to attract large numbers of ambitious musicians from around the world.

John has received many awards during his career, including a Fellowship of the Royal Academy of Music, two honorary Doctorates and, not least, the CBE – all in recognition of his services to music. He continues to travel widely – playing, conducting and composing – a tirelessly enthusiastic promoter of the music which has been the love of his life.